WATERWISE GARDEN

TOM MASSEY
WATERWISE GARDEN

Sustain
Your
Garden
Through
Drought
& Flood

FOREWORD

DR MARK GUSH
Head of Environmental Horticulture, Science and Collections Division
Royal Horticultural Society

Many years ago, I was encouraged by my professor of hydrology to go outside when it was raining and watch "hydrology in action". This was great advice, as it planted a seed of curiosity in me about the dynamics and cycling of water in the landscape. I have continued watching, and things are changing. Like me, anyone with the slightest interest in the vagaries of the weather will have noticed that rainfall is increasingly unpredictable. Whether it's deluge or drought, this is the new normal – the climate crisis is a water crisis.

I experienced this firsthand while living in the Western Cape of South Africa in 2018, where I was caught up in the alarming and unprecedented phenomenon of "Day Zero" – when the demand for water was predicted to imminently exceed supply, and Cape Town's taps would literally run dry. Restrictions were imposed and alternative water resources sought. Thankfully, with the collective efforts of the community to reduce water use and, by grace, the eventual return of good rainfall, the crisis was averted. The experience instilled improved water management practices into many South Africans, along with a heightened appreciation of the intrinsic value of water. We would all do well to heed these lessons to help prevent a similar crisis occurring in our own region. This book helpfully sets

Designed and planted to utilize rain, Tom Massey's WaterAid garden provides waterwise inspiration.

out water's value as a resource and tackles the challenges posed by a gardener's need for the right amount of water at the right time, in the face of growing demand and climate extremes.

What we plant and grow, and how we manage it, directly impacts the cycling of water above, on, and below ground. Cumulatively, small-scale changes, such as improved water management in gardens, can have significant benefits for water management in larger-scale systems. With this approach, there is substantial capacity within our gardens and green spaces to alleviate threats to people and the environment, such as flooding, heat stress, and drought, especially in an increasingly urbanized, impermeable, and warming world.

Few are more attuned to the reality of more intense rainfall and periods of drought than gardeners and horticulturists, for whom water is critical to their endeavours. In a changing climate we need this awareness, along with an adaptable mindset, so that we can better learn how to manage water responsibly in our green spaces, while maintaining their aesthetic beauty and the joy of gardening.

The Royal Horticultural Society (RHS) is actively researching and promoting ways to improve water management in our gardens and green spaces. This includes collecting, storing, and utilizing rainwater, slowing and reducing runoff, improving the retention and availability of water in soil, and understanding the water used by different plants. Striving to be more effective and efficient in the use of this precious resource is also part of Tom Massey's design ethos.

His sustainable gardens and landscapes support wildlife, promote biodiversity, and benefit their local environment; so much so that he was recently awarded a Gold Medal at the RHS Chelsea Flower Show for the WaterAid Garden, that demonstrated waterwise principles and practices. There is still a great deal for us all to learn about being waterwise, and this timely book provides a comprehensive and eminently practical guide to water management considerations for gardens and other areas of horticulture.

> Anyone with the slightest interest in the vagaries of the weather will have noticed that rainfall is increasingly unpredictable. Whether it's deluge or drought, this is the new normal – the climate crisis is a water crisis.

FOREWORD 004
A WATERWISE VISION 009

CHAPTER 1
WHY DO WE NEED TO BE WATERWISE?
012

CHAPTER 2
ACTIVE WATER HARVESTING
044

CHAPTER 3
PASSIVE WATER HARVESTING
072

CHAPTER 4
NURTURING YOUR SOIL
090

CHAPTER 5
THE WATERWISE GARDEN
106

CHAPTER 6
WATERWISE PLANTING
132

BIBLIOGRAPHY & RESOURCES	182
FURTHER READING	184
INDEX	186
ACKNOWLEDGEMENTS	190
ABOUT THE AUTHOR	192

GO.DK.COM/WATERWISE-GARDEN-UK

A WATERWISE VISION

As a landscape designer and passionate gardener, I have witnessed firsthand the growing impact of climate change on our gardens and green spaces. Each year seems to set new extremes, whether it's record-breaking summer heat or unprecedented winter rainfall, or both. Water – in excess or scarcity – is becoming a persistent challenge when designing and maintaining outside spaces.

Gardeners are acutely aware of the weather, always mindful of wet, dry, hot, or cool spells, and we adapt our practices accordingly. It is interesting to witness the varied ways that water can affect things: the very wet winter we had in 2023/24 in London, where I live and work, led to a boom in slug and snail activity, with many gardeners reporting feeling overrun as these creatures fed on plants in gardens and allotments. The wet also created a perfect breeding ground for fungal plant diseases. This was followed by a drier spring and summer growing season, which caused a boom in powdery mildew and other diseases, as plants became stressed by a lack of water. The impacts on gardens of the excessive rainfall and droughts that are already more common in a changing climate are more nuanced and complex than we might think.

[Above] Tom Massey explores waterwise methods in his innovative designs. **[Left]** Adaptable planting, selected to tolerate seasonal variations in water availability, in the Yeo Valley Organic garden, RHS Chelsea Flower Show 2021.

What we do in our gardens can also affect the wider environment, for example, hard, paved, impermeable gardens can cause runoff of heavy rainfall, which planted areas are much more capable of absorbing. In the more frequent extreme storms we are facing due to climate change (see pp.22–23), this runoff leads to sewer systems being overwhelmed, causing flooding and potential discharges of untreated sewage into our rivers and oceans (see pp.36–37).

Global reports of catastrophic weather events – devastating floods, crippling heatwaves, and uncontrolled wildfires – can no longer be ignored. All of these issues are water related, and influence the cycle of water across the globe (see pp.18–19). While this situation can feel overwhelming and insurmountable, I find solace in the knowledge that what I do as a landscape designer, and the choices I make in my own garden, can genuinely make a difference.

DESIGNING PRACTICAL SOLUTIONS

Through my work I have been exploring how we can design landscapes and gardens that are more waterwise (see the WaterAid garden p.40 and the waterwise garden p.106). This could involve: collecting rainfall to ease pressure on mains water systems; slowing the flow of water via landscape interventions to utilize rainwater and reduce runoff into sewer systems; or designing plant communities and nurturing precious soils to act like a sponge, helping to soak up downpours while providing benefits to ecosystems and boosting biodiversity.

All of these themes are explored in this book, and build upon waterwise ideas touched on in my first book, *RHS Resilient Garden*, which was all about gardening in the face of the climate emergency. This much deeper exploration into the subject, aims to demonstrate that waterwise interventions or changes to the way that we garden can, collectively, make a huge difference to the critical water situation we face (see p.14). Being more waterwise in our gardens can help reduce the risk of flooding, prevent hosepipe bans, free up potable water for drinking, sanitation, and hygiene, and prevent the alarming and genuine risk of a "day zero" event (as described by Mark Gush in his foreword), where water literally stops coming out of our taps.

Too often in landscape and garden design water is undervalued – just seen as waste to be flushed away. This book aims to rebrand it as a vital and precious resource that should not be wasted!

In the WaterAid garden, black birch (*Betula nigra*) forms a central feature in a planting zone designed to cope with flooding after heavy rainfall.

"WATERWISE INTERVENTIONS OR CHANGES TO THE WAY THAT WE GARDEN CAN, COLLECTIVELY, MAKE A HUGE DIFFERENCE TO THE CRITICAL WATER SITUATION WE FACE."

CHAPTER ONE

WHY DO WE NEED TO BE WATERWISE?

THE GLOBAL WATER CRISIS

WATER IS THE PLANET'S LIFEBLOOD, ESSENTIAL TO THE SURVIVAL OF ALL LIVING THINGS. THE UK, WHERE I LIVE AND WORK, IS AN ISLAND WITH FAMOUSLY WET WEATHER. BUT THE SHOCKING REALITY IS THAT IN JUST 25 YEARS EVEN AREAS HERE COULD FACE NOT HAVING ENOUGH WATER TO SUPPLY THEIR NEEDS.

Like many, I often take for granted my access to clean water, but this luxury is not available to everyone on the planet, and in the context of the climate emergency, it may well be something many more of us live without in the not too distant future. For communities in many parts of the world access to clean water is already scarce. Working with the charity WaterAid on a garden for RHS Chelsea Flower Show in 2024 (see pp.40–41) increased my awareness of these issues and really hit home to me the scale of the global water crisis.

Access to water and sanitation is a human right, recognized by the United Nations, however, billions of people globally are living without safely managed water. People in many parts of the world, primarily women and girls, have to walk miles to collect clean water for daily use. For those of us lucky enough to live with easy access to safe water and sanitation, it is hard to imagine how these issues might affect us, but even the water infrastructure of developed countries is not immune to the threats posed by underinvestment and a changing climate (see pp.16–17).

HUMAN RIGHTS TO WATER AND SANITATION

The United Nations recognizes access to water and sanitation as human rights.
- The right to water ensures access to sufficient, safe, affordable, and accessible water for personal use.
- The right to sanitation guarantees safe, hygienic, and affordable facilities that provide privacy, dignity, and cultural acceptability.

[Above] Women in the desert of Ethiopia must walk long distances carrying heavy containers filled with water, in hot and trying conditions.
[Right] Wasteful, untargeted watering with an oscillating sprinkler hose attachment demonstrates the lack of value that is so often placed on the clean water that comes out of our taps.

WHAT IS CAUSING GLOBAL WATER STRESS?

GLOBAL WATER DEMAND HAS MORE THAN DOUBLED SINCE 1960, WHILE THE PLANET'S POPULATION HAS BURGEONED FROM 3 BILLION TO 7.5 BILLION PEOPLE. TODAY, DEMAND FOR WATER CONSTANTLY EXCEEDS AVAILABLE RESOURCES AND AROUND 50 PER CENT OF THE WORLD'S POPULATION SUFFER HIGHLY WATER-STRESSED CONDITIONS FOR AT LEAST ONE MONTH EACH YEAR.

An ever-expanding population needs more water and food. This results in more intensive irrigated agriculture, increased livestock production, a higher demand for energy, and increased manufacturing: all of which need water. Compounding this pressure on water supplies is a lack of investment in water infrastructure. In the UK, for example, many sewers were built over 150 years ago, but are servicing a modern population far larger than they were designed for. They can also be overwhelmed by increased rainfall due to climate change. Ageing water infrastructure is not uncommon globally, and unsustainable water use policies, lack of education on water use, and increasingly extreme and unpredictable weather due to climate change, can all affect the available water supply.

Climate-related disasters, including drought, wildfires, and floods, are also all linked to rainfall and cause terrible pollution and huge economic impacts, as well as loss of biodiversity, habitat, and ecosystems. Climate change is now seriously affecting the weather, increasing the frequency and intensity of the storms and catastrophic weather events that contribute to such disasters. It is the most vulnerable communities around the world that are disproportionately affected.

Approximately 25 per cent of the global population faces extremely high water stress each year, with 25 countries using up almost their entire available water supply on a regular basis. Water stress detrimentally affects people's lives, jobs, and food and energy security. Water is central to farming, food production, power generation, and human health: a secure water supply is central to life.

WHAT IS WATER STRESS?

Water stress is the ratio of water demand to renewable supply. A country facing "extreme water stress" is using at least 80 per cent of its available supply, "high water stress" means it is withdrawing 40 per cent of its supply. The smaller the difference between supply and demand, the more vulnerable a population is to water shortages.

WATER CRISIS FACTS

Although the water crisis is global, it disproportionately affects the lives of people in the developing world, where a lack of clean water impacts health and opportunities.

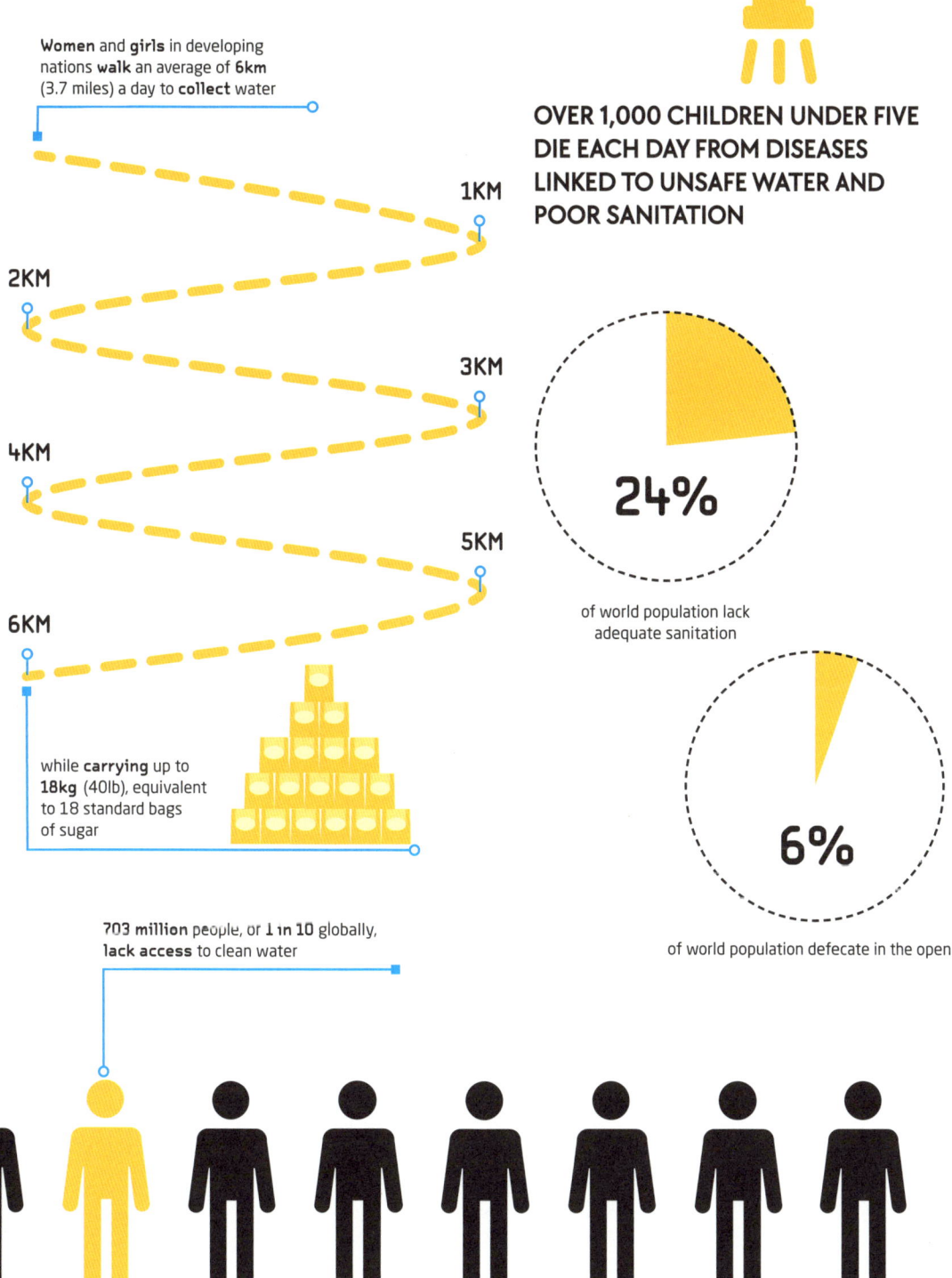

Women and **girls** in developing nations **walk** an average of **6km** (3.7 miles) a day to **collect** water

while **carrying** up to **18kg** (40lb), equivalent to 18 standard bags of sugar

703 million people, or **1 in 10** globally, **lack access** to clean water

OVER 1,000 CHILDREN UNDER FIVE DIE EACH DAY FROM DISEASES LINKED TO UNSAFE WATER AND POOR SANITATION

24% of world population lack adequate sanitation

6% of world population defecate in the open

017

THE WATER CYCLE AND CLIMATE CHANGE

THE WATER CYCLE DESCRIBES THE CONTINUOUS MOVEMENT OF WATER ON EARTH AS IT CIRCULATES THROUGH SOLID, LIQUID, AND VAPOUR STATES ON LAND, IN THE OCEANS, AND IN THE ATMOSPHERE. IT IS ESSENTIAL FOR SUSTAINING ALL LIFE ON EARTH, BUT IS SENSITIVE TO CHANGES IN OUR CLIMATE.

The global water cycle combines three major processes: evaporation, condensation, and precipitation. These govern the movement of surface water into the atmosphere, cloud formation, and rainfall, all of which are pivotal to weather systems and the availability of water for both human populations and natural ecosystems.

EVAPOTRANSPIRATION, CONDENSATION, AND PRECIPITATION

Evaporation occurs when water from the Earth's surface, for example in lakes, oceans, or soils, is heated up by the sun, turning it from a liquid to a gas. This water vapour then rises into the atmosphere, along with that from transpiration, which happens when plants take up liquid water from the soil via their roots and release it into the air from their leaves as vapour. The combined movement of water into the atmosphere is known as "evapotranspiration". Transpiration accounts for 61 per cent of evapotranspiration globally.

Condensation is the process where water vapour in the air turns into liquid water. This occurs when warm air cools and loses its capacity to hold moisture. Water vapour in the air returns to a liquid form, leading to the formation of clouds, fog, and dew. Clouds appear when water vapour in rising warm air cools and condenses around tiny dust or salt particles in the atmosphere. Transportation occurs when clouds are carried on wind and weather currents.

As more water vapour condenses, the cloud swells. Eventually, when more moisture accumulates than the air can hold, it falls back to Earth in liquid or solid form as precipitation, such as rain, hail, or snow.

Other processes involved in the water cycle include: runoff, or the movement of liquid water across land; interception, meaning the temporary storage of water on plants or buildings; and infiltration, the movement of water through soil.

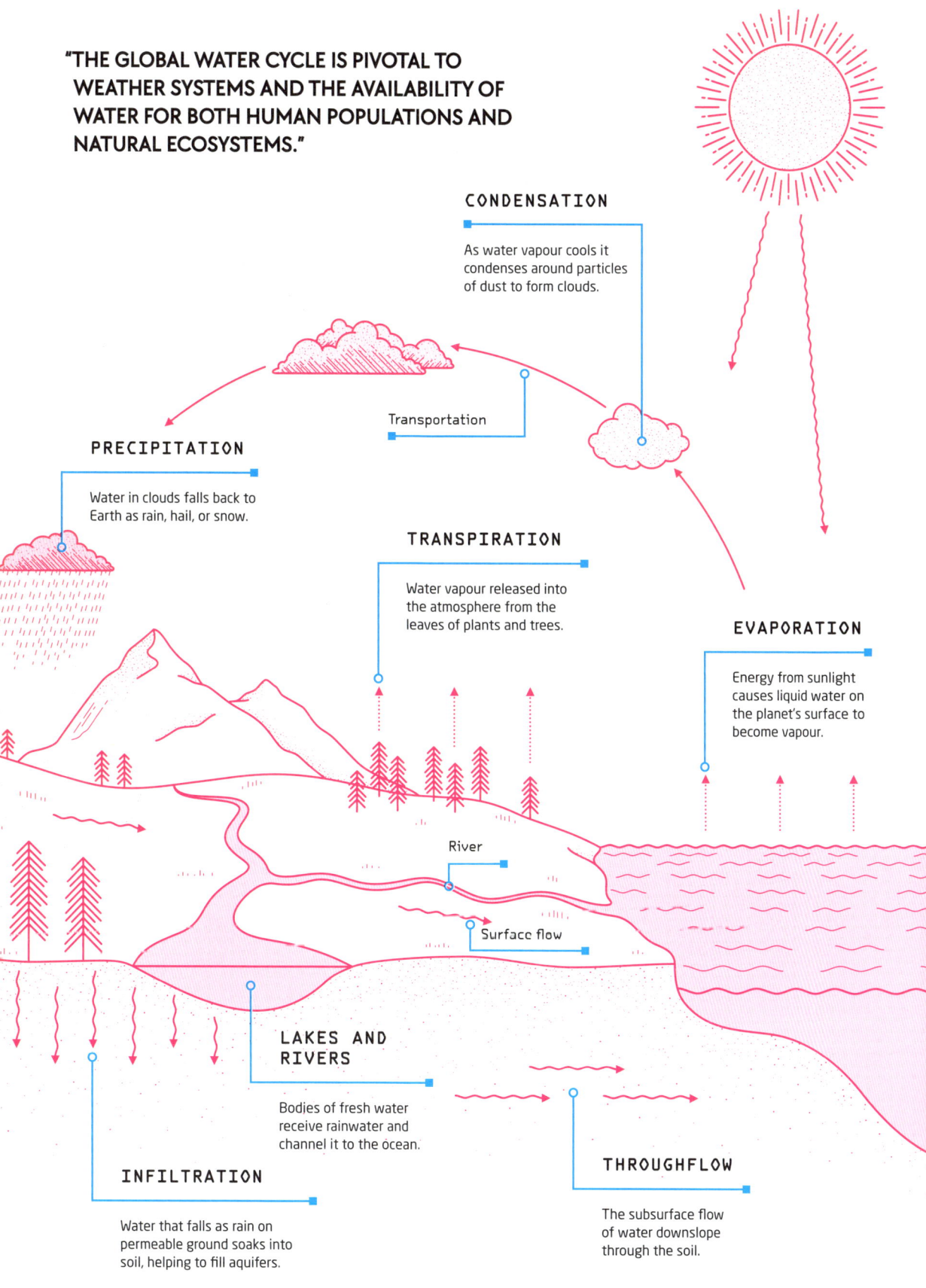

[Right] Urban flooding in Tulcea, Romania, followed heavy summer rainfall in July 2017.
[Far right] Winter storms in February 2014 caused widespread flooding across southern and western parts of the UK, including at Whitney-on-Wye, Herefordshire, where the River Wye burst its banks, inundating large swathes of surrounding farmland.

CLIMATE CHANGE'S IMPACT ON THE WATER CYCLE

There is a huge amount of evidence to suggest that climate change has significantly affected the Earth's water cycle. Activities like carbon emissions, agriculture, and industrialization have contributed to a rise in global temperatures, which have directly impacted key components of the water cycle, particularly evaporation, precipitation, and the movement of water worldwide.

As warming global temperatures accelerate evaporation rates, they also increase rates of precipitation. More moisture is held in warmer air: for every 1°C (1.8°F) the air warms, it can hold 7 per cent more water. This leads to more rainfall, but not necessarily in the areas where the extra water evaporated from – wind currents and global weather patterns tend to move clouds significant distances before precipitation occurs.

This shift in the water cycle has led to extreme weather events in recent years (see pp.22). While some regions are experiencing severe droughts, others face excessive rainfall. Rapid evaporation leads to quick condensation and intense storms, often resulting in flash floods, which are made worse by impermeable surfaces in urban areas.

Conversely, rising temperatures and increased evaporation rates are causing some larger water bodies to shrink. Lake Poopó in Bolivia dried up in 2015 due to drought, and Lake Mead, the reservoir formed by the Hoover Dam on the Colorado River in the southwestern United States, saw a dramatic 37m (120ft) drop in level from 2000 to 2015, because of higher temperatures and drought conditions.

TYPES OF FLOODING

- **Flash floods** Sudden accumulation of large amounts of water in an area.
- **Urban floods** Overwhelming of city drainage systems by heavy rainfall.
- **Riverbank and coastal flooding** Overflow of rivers, lakes, or seas caused by heavy precipitation and storm surges.

"MORE MOISTURE IS HELD IN WARMER AIR: FOR EVERY 1°C (1.8°F) THE AIR WARMS, IT CAN HOLD 7 PER CENT MORE WATER."

WORLD METEOROLOGICAL ORGANIZATION

EXTREME WEATHER

CLIMATE DATA AND OBSERVATIONS SHOW THAT, GLOBALLY, WEATHER IS BECOMING MORE EXTREME. THE FREQUENCY OF HEAVY RAINFALL AND HIGH TEMPERATURES HAS RISEN OVER RECENT DECADES, WHILE EXTREME COLD HAS DECLINED. SCIENTISTS ATTRIBUTE MUCH OF THIS SHIFT TO MANMADE CLIMATE CHANGE.

THE HUMAN FACTOR

Many factors combine to cause extreme weather events; some are natural, like the El Niño phenomenon, but others are caused by human activity, such as greenhouse gas emissions. How do we know if human activities are responsible for the changing weather? Scientists use historical weather data to assess the likelihood of extreme weather events before humans started burning fossil fuels. Computer models are also used to simulate the probability of extreme weather in worlds with and without climate change. This has shown that many, although not all, events are attributable to climate change, for example, that all heatwaves are now more likely and stronger.

AVERAGE GLOBAL TEMPERATURE RISE
The average surface temperature of the Earth has increased by a little over 1°C (1.8°F) during the past 100 years. This global warming causes hotter heatwaves, storms that are more intense, and changing precipitation patterns (more and less rainfall in different regions).

MORE INTENSE HEATWAVES
Heatwaves are becoming more frequent, longer lasting, and hotter. Record-breaking temperatures are being reached more often all over the globe, causing widespread damage to human populations and natural ecosystems.

INCREASINGLY HEAVY RAINFALL AND FLOODING
More moisture is held in warmer air, so global warming is resulting in heavier downpours, which increase the risk of flooding. Drainage systems don't have capacity to hold these large influxes of water and are overwhelmed increasingly frequently (see pp.34–35).

POWERFUL TROPICAL STORMS
The number of hurricanes, typhoons, and cyclones is not reported to be rising significantly, but the severity of these storms is increasing. As the oceans warm, they provide a greater source of energy for tropical storms, causing more extreme and damaging events.

DEVASTATING DROUGHTS
Changing precipitation patterns are causing prolonged droughts that are experienced by people across the world. Areas that were already prone to dryness are becoming drier still, while regions that used to have more balanced rain patterns are increasingly exposed to periods of drought.

WILDFIRES
Hotter, drier weather leads to an increased risk of wildfires, which are incredibly damaging and can rage out of control for months. Southern Europe, Australia, and California have all been affected by severe wildfire seasons in recent years, with burning lasting longer and affecting larger areas than before.

POLAR REGION CHANGES
The Arctic is warming at an alarming rate (more than double the rate of the rest of the world). This increased heat is melting sea ice, which is affecting global sea levels. On land, melting permafrost is also releasing a potent greenhouse gas – methane.

Wildfires are much more likely to start and spread through forest and brush in the tinder-dry conditions created by heatwaves and droughts.

ARE EXTREMES BECOMING MORE FREQUENT?

This graph plots the number of weather events resulting in loss of personal or business assets worldwide, and the upward trend is clear. Climate scientists have long predicted these changes and we are now feeling the effects. Vulnerable communities and ecosystems are more often affected, whether by economic disruption, damage to infrastructure, or losses of habitat and biodiversity.

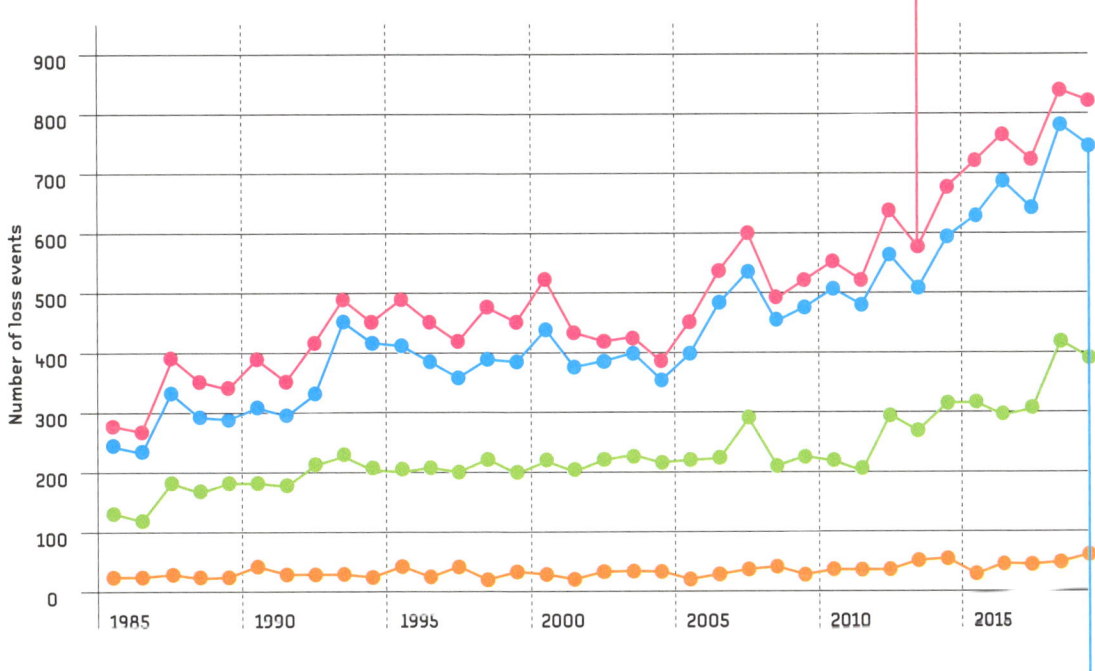

- Geophysical events: earthquake, tsunami, volcanic activity
- Meteorological events: tropical storm, convective storm, local storm
- Hydrological events: flood, landslide, rock fall
- Climatological events: extreme temperature, drought, wildfire

On 29 October 2024, Valencia, Spain received its usual annual rainfall in 24 hours. This devastating event caused flash floods, which turned streets into rivers, sweeping away cars, destroying buildings, and killing many people.

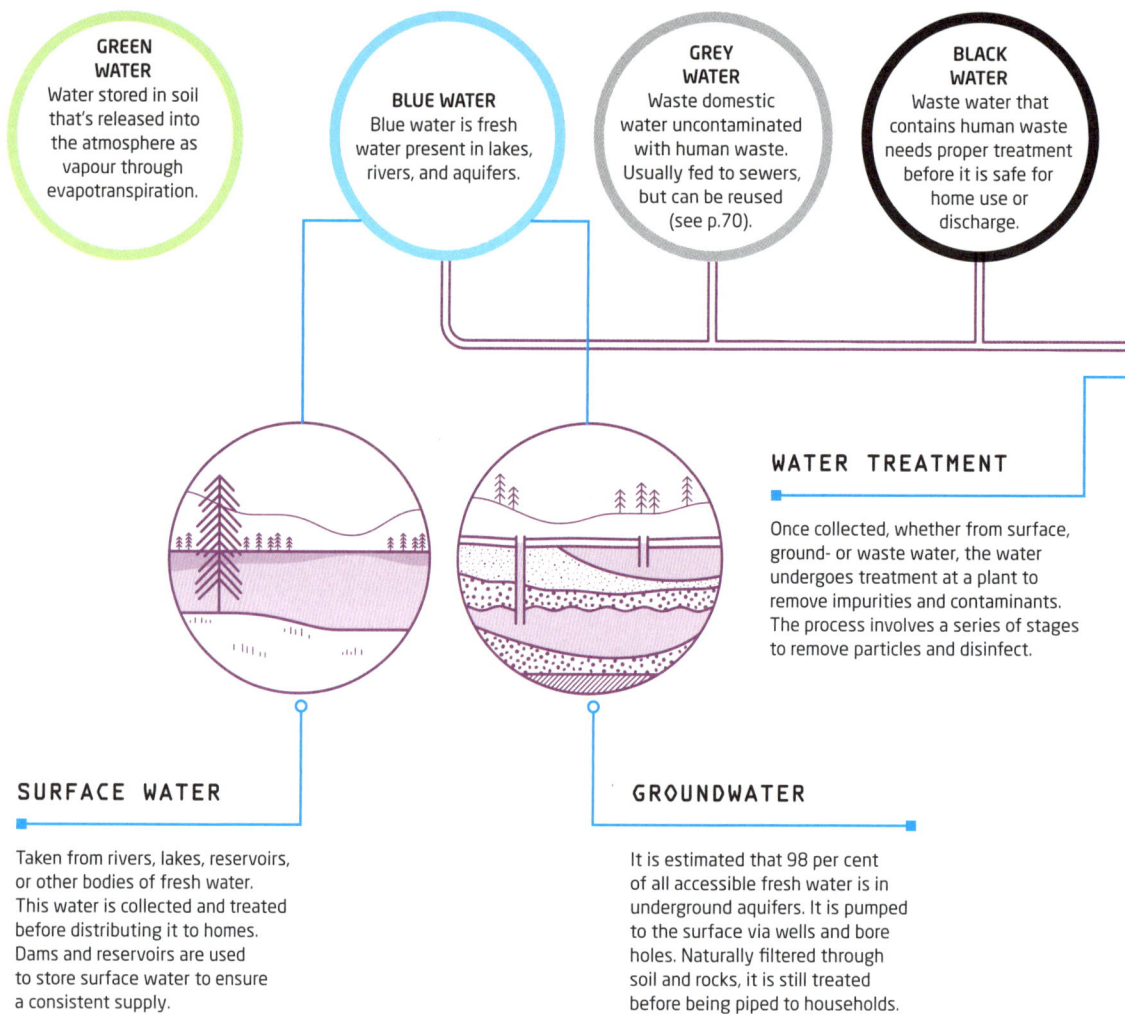

GREEN WATER
Water stored in soil that's released into the atmosphere as vapour through evapotranspiration.

BLUE WATER
Blue water is fresh water present in lakes, rivers, and aquifers.

GREY WATER
Waste domestic water uncontaminated with human waste. Usually fed to sewers, but can be reused (see p.70).

BLACK WATER
Waste water that contains human waste needs proper treatment before it is safe for home use or discharge.

WATER TREATMENT
Once collected, whether from surface, ground- or waste water, the water undergoes treatment at a plant to remove impurities and contaminants. The process involves a series of stages to remove particles and disinfect.

SURFACE WATER
Taken from rivers, lakes, reservoirs, or other bodies of fresh water. This water is collected and treated before distributing it to homes. Dams and reservoirs are used to store surface water to ensure a consistent supply.

GROUNDWATER
It is estimated that 98 per cent of all accessible fresh water is in underground aquifers. It is pumped to the surface via wells and bore holes. Naturally filtered through soil and rocks, it is still treated before being piped to households.

WHERE DOES MY TAP WATER COME FROM?

IF YOU ASK MOST PEOPLE WHERE THEIR WATER COMES FROM, THE ANSWER WILL PROBABLY BE: MY TAP! BUT NOT MANY OF US KNOW WHERE OUR TAP WATER ORIGINATES. WHERE DO WATER COMPANIES GET THIS WATER FROM AND HOW IS IT PROCESSED BEFORE IT'S READY TO COME OUT OF OUR TAPS?

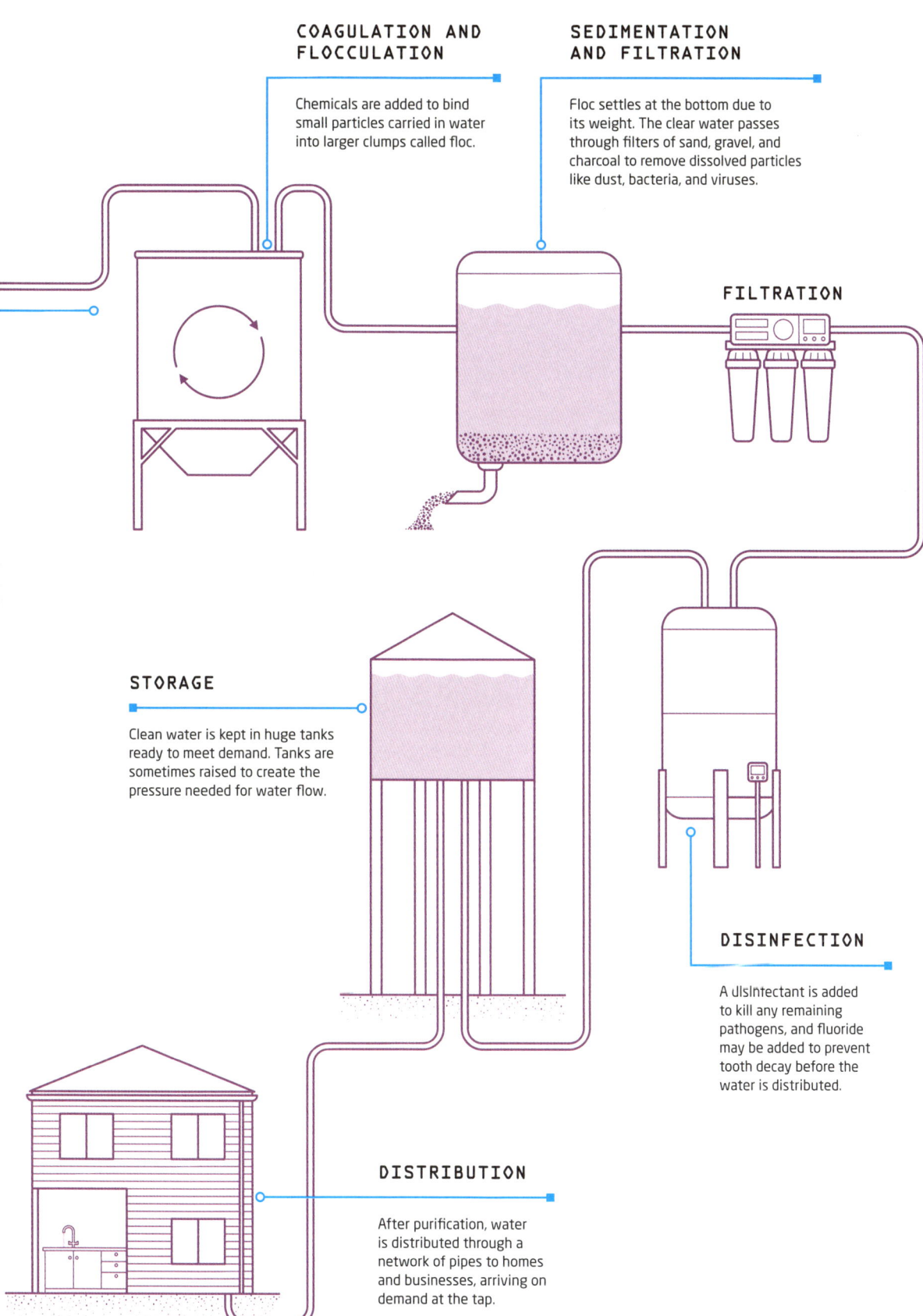

PHYSICAL WATER SCARCITY

When a region's demand for water has outpaced the available supply, this is known as physical water scarcity, which is linked to water stress (see p.16).

It is estimated that around 1.2 billion people live in areas of physical scarcity, often these are in arid or semi-arid regions. Arid regions receive less than 25cm (10in) of rain per year. Semi-arid regions receive 25–50cm (10–20in) of rain per year. Physical water scarcity can be seasonal, for example during hot and dry summer months. As the global population increases and the weather becomes more unpredictable and extreme, the number of people affected by physical water scarcity will increase too. By 2030, seven regions in England are projected to face severe water stress.

ECONOMIC WATER SCARCITY

Economic water scarcity is caused by a lack of water infrastructure, or infrastructure that is not fit for purpose. It can also result from poor management and maintenance where sufficient infrastructure is in place. In areas prone to economic water scarcity there usually is sufficient water to meet the region's needs, but access is somehow limited or the accessible water is polluted or unsanitary, making it unavailable.

Research from the United Nations Food and Agriculture Organization (FAO) estimates that more than 1.6 billion people face economic water scarcity. Residents of major cities, such as Mexico City and Johannesburg, already find their taps frequently running dry. In these situations, physical and economic water scarcity often reinforce each other; climate change is likely to push economically vulnerable regions closer to crisis by intensifying water shortages and reducing resilience to water-related stress.

Another significant problem is "non-revenue water", where treated water piped by water companies is lost before it reaches the consumer's tap through

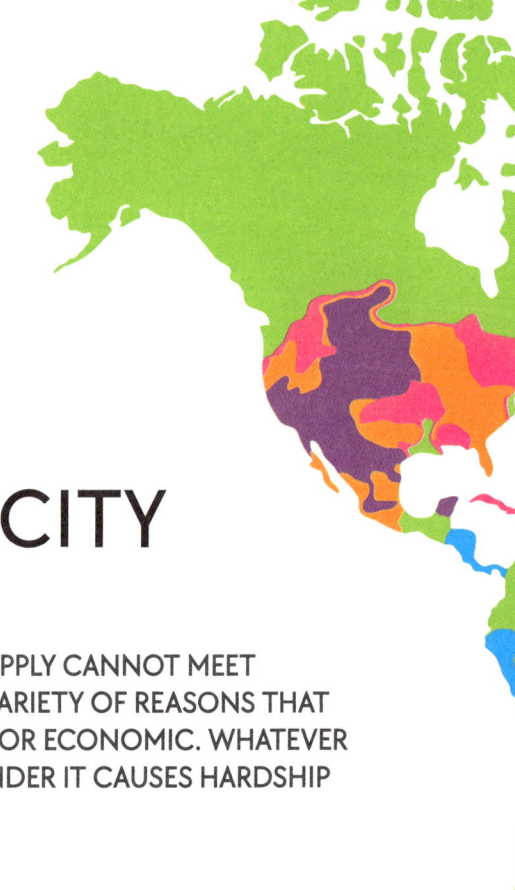

WATER SCARCITY

WATER SCARCITY OCCURS WHEN SUPPLY CANNOT MEET DEMAND. THIS CAN HAPPEN FOR A VARIETY OF REASONS THAT ARE CLASSIFIED AS EITHER PHYSICAL OR ECONOMIC. WHATEVER HEADING WATER SCARCITY FALLS UNDER IT CAUSES HARDSHIP FOR THE POPULATIONS AFFECTED.

leaking pipes or inefficient systems. In the US and the UK, non-revenue water averages around one-fifth of all treated water produced – a huge waste of resources and loss of potable water.

Major inefficiencies in water use, including excessive or unregulated extraction of water for manufacturing or agriculture, or due to a population undervaluing water as a finite natural resource, can also contribute to economic water scarcity.

WATER AND THE THREAT TO WORLD PEACE

The UN World Water Development Report 2024 outlines that access to clean water is critical to promoting world peace. It warns that increasing global water scarcity is fuelling conflicts, contributing to instability, and fanning the flames of geopolitical tensions. As populations increase and the effects of climate change are felt, this is only set to get worse.

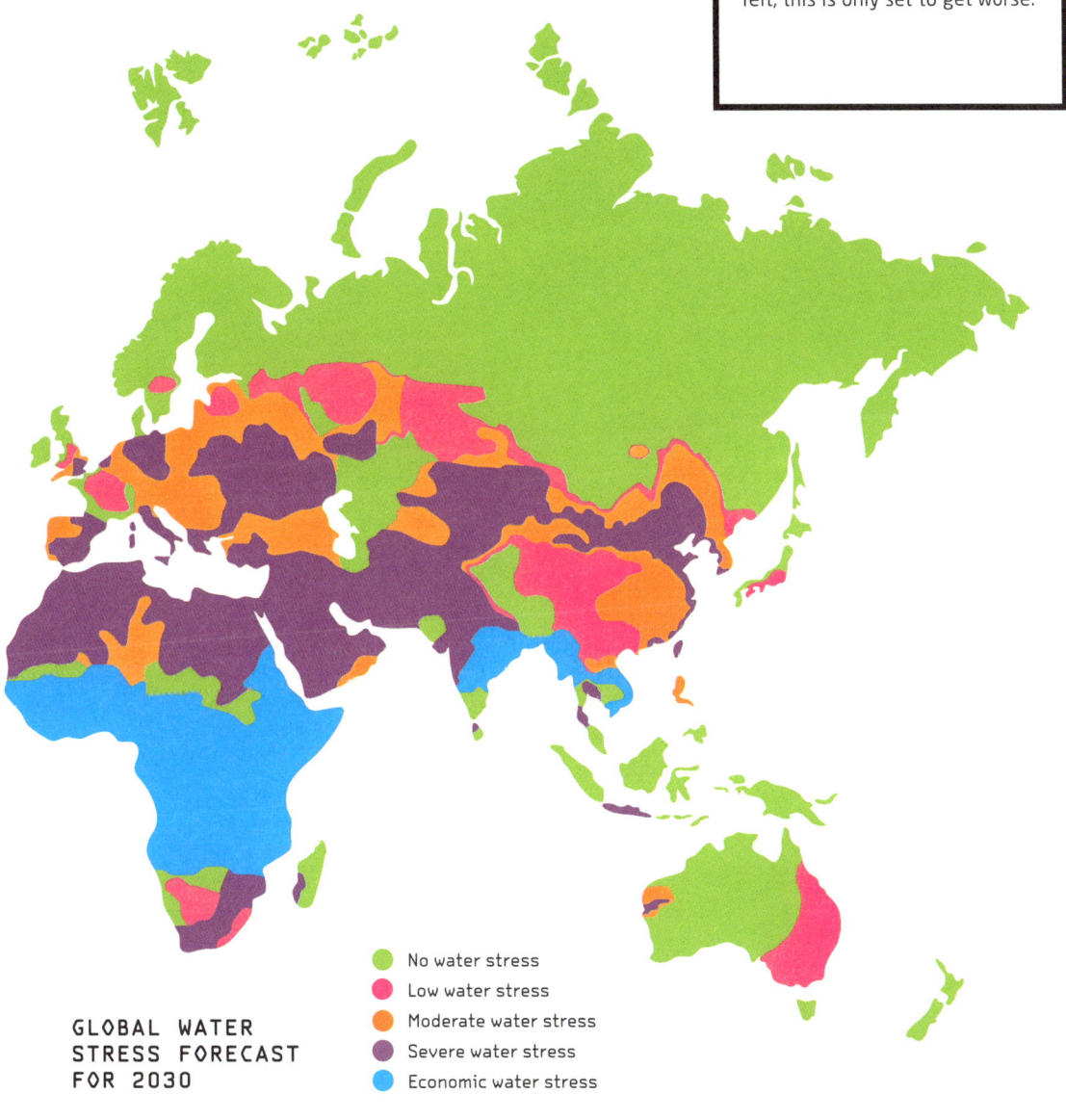

GLOBAL WATER STRESS FORECAST FOR 2030

- No water stress
- Low water stress
- Moderate water stress
- Severe water stress
- Economic water stress

HOW IS THIS RELEVANT TO GARDENS AND GARDENERS?

IN AN ERA OF CLIMATE CHANGE, PRESSURES ON WATER RESOURCES WILL ONLY INCREASE. THE CHALLENGE IS TO MAKE OUR GARDENS AND THE WAY WE MAINTAIN THEM MORE WATERWISE, SO THAT THEY ARE PART OF THE SOLUTION RATHER THAN PART OF THE PROBLEM.

In London, where I garden and grow, we are facing hosepipe bans more regularly thanks to hotter, drier summers, and we are experiencing more frequent and extreme heatwaves. In January 2022, the UK Climate Change Committee predicted that there was a "small chance" of temperatures reaching 40°C (104°F) in England before 2040 – London then hit 40°C (104°F) that July. We gardeners are still seeing the repercussions of that extreme July 2022 heatwave, with many plants and trees suffering slow decline after the shock of experiencing extreme heat that they are not adapted to withstand.

TAP WATER IS TOO PRECIOUS FOR PLANTS

Seasonal changes in water availability are a big part of the problem: water is not always abundant when it is most needed. Winters may be wet, but it is during the hotter, drier summers that demand for water rises dramatically. Watering the trees, plantings, and lawns in our gardens and public green spaces creates a big drain on water supplies during summer. Treated mains water is often used for this purpose, which is unnecessary, as plants actually prefer untreated rainwater (see p.39). Collecting and storing rainwater for irrigation is a simple change that can significantly reduce water consumption (see pp.44–71).

DESIGN CAN CREATE RESILIENCE

The way we design the hard landscaping in our outside spaces is also vitally important. Hard, impermeable surfaces like patios, driveways, and terraces contribute to surface water runoff, which can lead to localized flooding and sewage systems being overwhelmed (see pp.36–37). We can rethink this and adapt paved and impermeable areas (see pp.72–89) to create gardens that can act like sponges; supplying plants with the water they need, replenishing groundwater, and helping to prevent the economic and environmental damage caused by flooding and discharges of raw sewage into waterways. We also need to take the opportunity to rethink which plants to include in our gardens. Choosing those that are well adapted to the growing conditions in each area will allow them to flourish without the need for watering. It is also possible to find plants that are resilient enough to survive more extreme events, like floods or heatwaves, where these might occur.

Seasonal changes in water availability are a big part of the problem: water is not always abundant when it is most needed. Winters may be wet, but lengthening growing seasons and hotter, drier summers increase the demand for water.

[01] Increasingly frequent droughts and heatwaves can cause stress to plants that are not resilient to such harsh conditions, leaving them unable to thrive. [02] Gardeners need to reduce wasteful use of mains water and instead make use of collected rainwater.

[03] Unusually hot and dry weather resulted in low water levels in Lady Bower reservoir in the Peak District, UK, putting supplies under pressure. [04] A streak of brown foam floating on the surface of Belfast Lough, Northern Ireland, is a visible sign of overflow from sewage systems after heavy rain.

WHAT CAN GARDENERS DO?

AS GARDENERS, WE RELY ON WATER TO KEEP OUR PLANTS THRIVING, BUT THERE IS MUCH WE CAN DO TO BE MORE WATERWISE AND REDUCE PRESSURE ON LOCAL WATER SUPPLIES. THE ANSWER IS TO REDUCE USE OF MAINS TAP WATER AND TO WORK WITH NATURE TO STOP USING IT ALTOGETHER IN OUR GARDENS.

Natural systems constantly recycle and purify fresh water through the water cycle (see pp.18–19). Gardeners can support this cycle, and save money where water is metered, by designing waterwise gardens and adopting maintenance practices that recharge groundwater, regenerate ecosystems, and revitalize water sources, like wetlands.

THE PRINCIPLES OF WATERWISE GARDENING
Waterwise gardening relies on four fundamental principles to optimize water use. These are:
- Capturing and storing rainwater (see pp.44–71).
- Slowing water flow naturally (see pp.72–89).
- Improving soil health to maximize water absorption and retention (see pp.90–105).
- Choosing plants to suit local conditions (see pp.132–181).

My aim is to explain how to use these principles in every home and garden to reduce the need for watering and reliance on treated tap water. Each chapter will provide the tools and resources that should form the foundation of any garden or landscape that aspires to be waterwise.

It is easy to be daunted by the scale of the problem, or to feel anxiety when reading that water supplies may run out. But I find it useful to remember that every small thing we do individually can be part of a movement to tackle these issues. If we all commit to being more waterwise in our homes and gardens, collectively we can make a huge contribution to conserving this key resource.

BE MORE WATERWISE IN THE HOME

In the UK, the average person uses around 145 litres (32 gallons) of water per day, about 5 per cent of which is used outdoors. The rest is used indoors for activities such as toilet flushing, showering, and filling washing machines. Six simple steps can significantly reduce water usage:

- Turn off the tap while brushing your teeth or washing dishes.
- Take shorter showers and consider using a water-saving showerhead.
- Install dual-flush toilets to reduce water use per flush.
- Only run washing machines when full or use eco settings to reduce water per load.
- Fix leaking taps, which can waste thousands of litres per year.
- Install aerators on taps to reduce flow without sacrificing water pressure.

[Top] A swale, designed as an attractive feature to hold water in the landscape and help recharge groundwater, was part of my design for the WaterAid Garden at RHS Chelsea Flower Show.
[Left] A metal trough receives and stores rainwater from a roof, preventing it running into mains sewers. Open storage tanks can look good, but not covering water does present risks (see p.53).

WATERWISE TIPS FOR A SUSTAINABLE GARDEN

ADOPT THESE TEN SIMPLE, PRACTICAL STEPS IN ANY GARDEN TO HELP PROTECT VITAL POTABLE WATER SUPPLIES. EMBRACING WATERWISE PRACTICES ALLOWS YOU TO MAINTAIN A VIBRANT, HEALTHY GARDEN THAT IS MORE SUSTAINABLE, BUT ALSO MORE RESILIENT TO CHANGING WEATHER PATTERNS, AND BENEFICIAL TO THE LOCAL ENVIRONMENT.

DISCONNECT YOUR DOWNPIPES

Redirecting downpipes allows you to harvest rainwater for use in your garden, while also helping to prevent stormwater runoff causing local flooding or overloading the sewer system (see pp.36–37).

INSTALL A WATER BUTT OR RAINWATER HARVESTING TANK

Collecting rainwater provides a free water source that is a valuable alternative to tap water, which is better for plants, as it's low in minerals and free from chemical additives (see p.39).

Robert Bray Associates playfully divert a downpipe into a planter via a watering can.

COVER SOIL WITH A MULCH

Adding a mulch, such as chipped bark, homemade compost, or gravel, to the soil surface (see p.94) allows rain through, while limiting temperature extremes and the evaporation of soil moisture, reducing the need to water.

ADD ORGANIC MATTER TO SOIL

Adding organic matter to soil, ideally homemade compost, improves its structure and helps it retain moisture (see pp.100–103). This makes it easier for plants to access moisture without additional watering.

LESS PAVING, MORE PLANTS

Planted areas allow water to soak into soil, replenishing groundwater supplies and creating healthy ecosystems, whereas impermeable paved surfaces cause stormwater runoff, which can overwhelm sewer systems (see pp.36-37). Plants also have a cooling effect on the area around them.

CHOOSE THE RIGHT PLANT FOR THE RIGHT PLACE, FOR THE RIGHT PURPOSE

Selecting plants suited to the specific conditions in different areas of your garden minimizes the need for watering. "Hydrozoning", or grouping plants with similar water needs together, makes watering more efficient (see p.135). Plants can also be chosen for specific purposes, like stabilizing soil, or absorbing flood water.

Paving with planted channels, laid on a permeable sub-base, allows water to percolate into the ground below.

USE PERMEABLE PAVING

Opt for hard surfaces that allow water to soak into the ground and reduce runoff, such as gravel, porous pavers, or decking (see p.88). Existing paving can also be made permeable (see pp.120-121).

USE A WATERING CAN

Targeted watering of specific plants with a can is more efficient than using hoses or sprinklers, and is the easiest way to make use of stored rainwater (see p.46). A hose can use around 1,000 litres (220 gallons) of water per hour, the equivalent to one person's water use for a whole week.

MAINS TO RAINS

The RHS and Cranfield University have created a website called "Mains to Rains", which aims to help gardeners reduce their reliance on mains water, become more climate resilient, and use water more effectively and efficiently. Visit the website to find out more and join other gardeners by pledging to switch to watering with rainwater and to adopt various practical and easy-to-implement changes in your own garden.

mains2rains.uk

DON'T WATER YOUR LAWN

Lawns are surprisingly resilient, especially when permitted to grow longer. Allow grass to turn brown in dry spells – it will turn green again with rain. Regular watering and close mowing both promote shallow roots, making a lawn less drought tolerant.

PLACE DRIP TRAYS UNDER POTS

Plants in pots rely on watering. Use drip trays to catch excess water, allowing compost and roots to absorb it, rather than letting it drain away. Open soil retains moisture far better than compost in pots, so consider planting in the soil where possible.

WHY DO WE NEED TO BE WATERWISE?

SUSTAINABLE WATER USE

JANET MANNING has worked at "both ends of the hose", at Wessex Water and a production nursery. As Garden Water Scientist at Cranfield University she helped create the Mains to Rains pledges. She is now RHS Water Reduction Officer.

Edible Bristol's allotment site has provided Janet Manning with the ideal opportunity to test the impact of the sustainable water use pledges recommended by Mains to Rains.

DO GARDENS AND GARDENING HAVE AN IMPORTANT ROLE TO PLAY IN MAKING OUR WATER USE SUSTAINABLE?

Nothing grows without water. Gardens may not consume large volumes of water compared to flushing toilets, but they are the place where we can understand how we can help repair the water cycle by getting more rain into soils. When soils work well, they maintain a healthy balance of oxygen and water in the root zone and plants are able to thrive through both wet and dry spells. Once we understand how water and oxygen move through soils, rain gardening concepts are much simpler to implement and we can all become better growers.

MAINS TO RAINS SEEKS TO PROVIDE SIMPLE, ACTIONABLE WATERWISE ADVICE, WHAT HAS THE UPTAKE BEEN LIKE?

Mains to Rains (see p.33) has received 3,646 pledges from UK gardeners, with water butts and mulching the most frequently pledged actions. Although over 2,000 gardeners pledged to use a water butt, the pledges to improve soil health and structure are actually more valuable, because they allow more rain to infiltrate and attenuate in the soil, saving more than 100 times the amount that would fit into 2,000 water butts. Rainfall is stored by using organic mulches, choosing the right plants for the right place, and using self-watering pots that collect rainwater. It's about changing cultivation practices so that the rain lasts through to the next rainfall. Deeply aerated soil is the natural world's water butt.

YOU USE THE TERM "ATTENUATION". CAN YOU EXPLAIN WHAT THIS MEANS?

Soils and plants naturally attenuate rainfall like a sponge; in other words they hold onto the water and clean it by filtering out particles and dissolved nutrients, and then release it gradually. If you have soil in your garden, the chances are it is attenuating far more rainwater than you could ever hope to fit into a water butt.

HOW WERE THE EFFECTS OF MAINS TO RAINS PLEDGES MEASURED AT EDIBLE BRISTOL'S ALLOTMENTS. WHAT WERE THE RESULTS?

I volunteer at Edible Bristol (EB) with Sara Venn and her community gardeners and found that they had been practising Mains to Rains advice before I had thought about it. It was the perfect place to test its effectiveness, so over the summer of 2023 every watering can filled was counted. Their organic mulches, minimal digging, rainwater harvesting, and targeted watering of root zones meant that although EB occupied 10 per cent of the site and had the largest polytunnel, their water use was only five per cent of allotment site's total. Next, we hope to collect rainwater from the roof of a neighbouring apartment building to reduce mains water use.

DISCONNECT YOUR DOWNPIPES

RAINWATER THAT FALLS ONTO A ROOF IS USUALLY CHANNELLED AWAY THROUGH GUTTERS AND DOWNPIPES, INTO A SEWER SYSTEM. SEVERING THE CONNECTION BETWEEN A DOWNPIPE AND THE SEWERS ALLOWS THIS PRECIOUS RAINWATER TO BE USED, AND CAN ALSO HELP TO PROTECT WATERWAYS FROM SEWAGE POLLUTION.

First it's important to understand where rainwater goes. Some sewage systems are split into clean, useful rainwater (green water, see p.24), and waste water from household use, such as toilets, bathrooms, and kitchens (grey and black water, see p.24). This is ideal as the dirty waste water is not mixed with the clean rainwater. In the UK and in many other parts of the world, however, most sewer systems are combined, meaning that clean water is mixed with dirty water, which all then needs processing before it can be useful again.

A SYSTEM DESIGNED TO DISCHARGE SEWAGE

During heavy rainfall, which is exacerbated by climate change, the capacity of combined sewer systems is sometimes exceeded. This can lead to inundation of sewage works, flooding, and in the worst cases, backing up of sewage into open spaces and homes. To combat this, combined sewer overflows were developed as pressure release valves, to reduce the risk of sewage backing up during heavy rainfall. They discharge into rivers and oceans, meaning that raw sewage is dumped into natural bodies of water. Water companies are often accused of using these overflows too frequently, causing harm to the environment, damaging fragile ecosystems, and risking the health of swimmers who bathe in the polluted water.

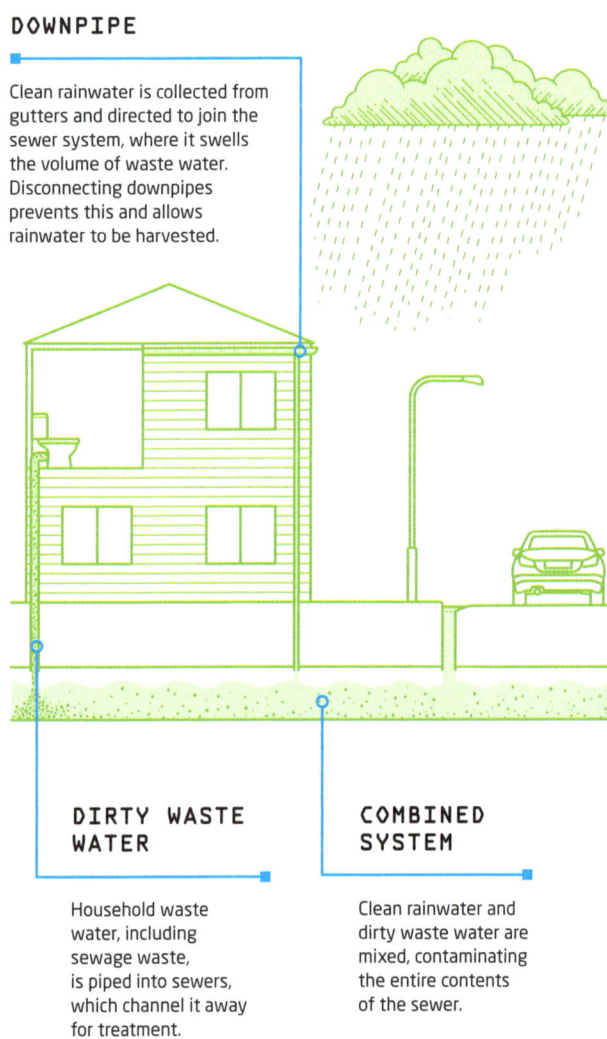

DOWNPIPE

Clean rainwater is collected from gutters and directed to join the sewer system, where it swells the volume of waste water. Disconnecting downpipes prevents this and allows rainwater to be harvested.

DIRTY WASTE WATER

Household waste water, including sewage waste, is piped into sewers, which channel it away for treatment.

COMBINED SYSTEM

Clean rainwater and dirty waste water are mixed, contaminating the entire contents of the sewer.

MAKE USE OF RAINWATER

By disconnecting our downpipes and utilizing or storing rainwater, we can stop it entering these combined sewer systems, and reduce the risk of raw sewage being discharged into our waterways and oceans. We can also use the rainwater for purposes like irrigating, planting, providing habitat, and creating interesting garden features such as rain gardens, swales, and ephemeral wildlife ponds (see pp.78–87). Utilizing rainwater saves money as it is quite literally a free resource that falls from the sky with no meter. Its use also takes pressure off mains water supplies, meaning that the treated potable water that comes out of your tap can just be used for drinking, hygiene, and sanitation.

SURFERS AGAINST SEWAGE

Surfers Against Sewage is one of the UK's most successful marine conservation and campaigning charities. They campaign against unlawful discharges of sewage and provide a helpful app that shows where discharges may have occurred, warning bathers and surfers not to swim while there is a risk of raw sewage in the water.

STORM DRAIN

Runoff from hard surfaces, like roads or drives, is directed into sewers to prevent flooding.

RAINWATER

Climate change is causing an increase in heavy rainfall, sometimes capable of overwhelming sewer systems. Harvesting rainwater helps to prevent this by reducing the amount of water entering sewers.

SEWER OUTFLOW

Stormwater polluted with sewage is discharged into rivers and oceans when heavy rainfall overloads the combined sewer system.

WATER FOR TREATMENT

Once combined, useful rainwater and dirty waste water must both be treated at a sewage works before being safe to use or discharge. This is wasteful of resources.

POLLUTED WATER

Water discharged from combined sewer systems harms aquatic life and makes river or sea water unsafe for swimming and water sports.

WATER HARVESTING

CAPTURING AND UTILIZING FREELY AVAILABLE WATER SOURCES IN YOUR GARDEN IS KNOWN AS WATER HARVESTING. THIS IS AN EFFECTIVE WAY TO REDUCE YOUR RELIANCE ON MAINS WATER AND ENHANCE WATER ACCESSIBILITY DURING DRY SPELLS, WHILE ALSO HELPING TO PROTECT THE LOCAL ENVIRONMENT FROM FLOODING.

Active rainwater harvesting (see pp.44–69) makes use of tanks or water butts to collect water for use, which need human input to access and manage stored water. This old wooden barrel is an attractive reclaimed option for harvesting rainwater.

COLLECTING RAINWATER

As gardeners, it's essential that we reduce our dependence on mains-supplied potable water for irrigation (see p.28) in order to preserve this vital resource. Generally it's best to start collecting the most readily available form of water. Rainfall is free and abundant in many regions, but is often undervalued and underutilized. It can be collected in a variety of ways, from simple water butts to more complex underground rainwater harvesting tanks and irrigation systems. The different methods used are divided into "active" rainwater harvesting, which is the collection and storage of rainfall so that it is available for use when needed, and "passive" rainwater harvesting, which includes a range of gravity-based systems designed to irrigate planted areas, infiltrate rainwater into the soil, and recharge groundwater supplies. I employed both of these methods to highlight the importance of sustainable water management in the design of the WaterAid garden (see pp.40–43).

WATER SOURCES AVAILABLE FOR HARVESTING

- **Rainwater** The most plentiful and accessible source for collection when it falls on roofs.
- **Stormwater** Rainwater that has already reached the ground and flows across surfaces, such as street runoff.
- **Grey water** Reusable household waste water not containing human waste, typically from sinks, showers, and baths.
- **Condensate and dew** Airborne moisture that condenses on surfaces cooler than the surrounding air.
- **Snow and fog** Only practical where weather conditions are suitable, mostly in mountainous or coastal regions.

WHY DO PLANTS PREFER RAINWATER?

Rainwater is naturally "soft" and low in dissolved minerals. The "hard" tap water in some areas contains high levels of minerals, such as calcium and magnesium, which can accumulate in soil or potting compost when plants are regularly watered. This build up, along with chemicals from the treatment process, can damage plant health. Using soft rainwater to water plants avoids any problems. Rainwater also has a pH of 5.5–6.5, which is lower than the pH of tap water. This is useful to plants because at this level the key plant nutrient phosphorus becomes soluble in water and can readily be taken up from the soil by roots.

Passive water harvesting (see pp.72–89) uses gravity, landscape interventions, earthworks, vegetation, and soil life to naturally capture, infiltrate, store, and reuse water – primarily rainwater and stormwater. Once established, passive systems, such as this dry gravel swale designed by Richard McPherson, function independently but can be improved with regular observation and maintenance.

"RAINFALL IS FREE AND ABUNDANT IN MANY REGIONS, BUT IS OFTEN UNDERVALUED AND UNDERUTILIZED."

CASE STUDY

THE WATERAID GARDEN Designed in collaboration with Je Ahn of Studio Weave, to harness rainwater and highlight the importance of sustainable water management in a changing climate, the WaterAid garden was showcased at the RHS Chelsea Flower Show in 2024, where it won a Gold Medal.

WHAT IS WATERAID?

WaterAid is an international not-for-profit organization, determined to make clean water, decent toilets, and good hygiene normal for everyone, everywhere. Their practical projects bring these basic human rights to communities in 22 countries worldwide. Meanwhile their campaigning and work with national and local governments raises awareness, support, and funding for the provision of clean water projects.

[Left] Adaptable, resilient, and alluring, this garden is designed to capture and make use of every drop of rainwater that falls on the space.

[Left] Dry and exposed, the planted roof suits plants such as sea thrift (*Armeria maritima*) and Mexican fleabane (*Erigeron karvinskianus*), that are well adapted to cope without irrigation.
[Below] Inspired by WaterAid's work in areas of drought, the rainwater harvesting pavilion is designed to collect, filter, and store rainwater.

The WaterAid garden addresses the challenges presented as our climate changes and water scarcity and insecurity become more commonplace, both in the UK and around the world. We can all do things to help mitigate climate change, such as improving soil health, planting greenery to cool the air and provide shade, and, most importantly, managing water sustainably.

The design focuses on sustainable water management, utilizing every drop of rainfall that lands on the space by capturing and storing it the striking, funnel-shaped central pavilion, or in the surrounding swales and ponds. All of the hard landscaping in the design is permeable, allowing water to percolate through into the soil below. Steel and timber decks float over the landscape, so that water, plants, and wildlife can move freely beneath them. Rainwater is also absorbed by the planted areas, which are filled with colourful plant species that have been carefully chosen to suit the varying amounts of soil moisture available to their roots in each distinct area of the design.

The centrepiece of the adaptable landscape design is the rainwater-harvesting pavilion. Its organic shape is strong and light, maximizing its roof surface area to efficiently collect rainfall. The four linked funnel-like structures contain filters that remove debris before channelling rainwater from the roof to underground storage tanks. The areas beneath the arches provide valuable, cooling shade from the hot sun. All of these functions are inspired by WaterAid's work with communities around the world to develop sustainable water solutions.

WHY DO WE NEED TO BE WATERWISE?

RECLAIMED MATERIALS

Wherever possible, the garden reuses, and even makes features of, reclaimed materials such as the repurposed steel walkway gratings.

A DESIGN FOR A CHANGING CLIMATE

The message of the WaterAid garden is one of hope, showing how resilience and innovation can help us all to adapt and flourish in the face of the climate crisis. The design encourages us to think about ways to conserve water and incorporate elements of rainwater harvesting into their own gardens, demonstrating how a resilient and beautiful garden can be achieved, whatever the future holds.

The WaterAid garden was possible through support from the grant-giving charity Giving Back and now has a permanent home at the National Trust's Castlefield Viaduct in Manchester, where it is open to the public. Study the design on this page, and perhaps visit to explore imaginative ways to use water in your garden more sustainably.

PLANTING

Planted areas permit water to infiltrate into soil. Plants chosen to suit the varied growing conditions reduce the need for watering.

EARTHWORKS

Soil excavated to make the water-filled ponds and depressions is used to form mounds, where the dry conditions suit different plants.

MANAGING RUNOFF

The undulations channel rainwater and slow its flow, allowing it to infiltrate into the soil, reducing runoff and soil erosion.

"THE CLIMATE CRISIS IS ALSO A WATER CRISIS. A STAGGERING 90% OF ALL NATURAL DISASTERS ARE WATER-RELATED, WITH MORE FREQUENT AND EXTREME FLOODS POLLUTING WATER SOURCES, AND DROUGHTS DRYING UP SPRINGS."

WATERAID

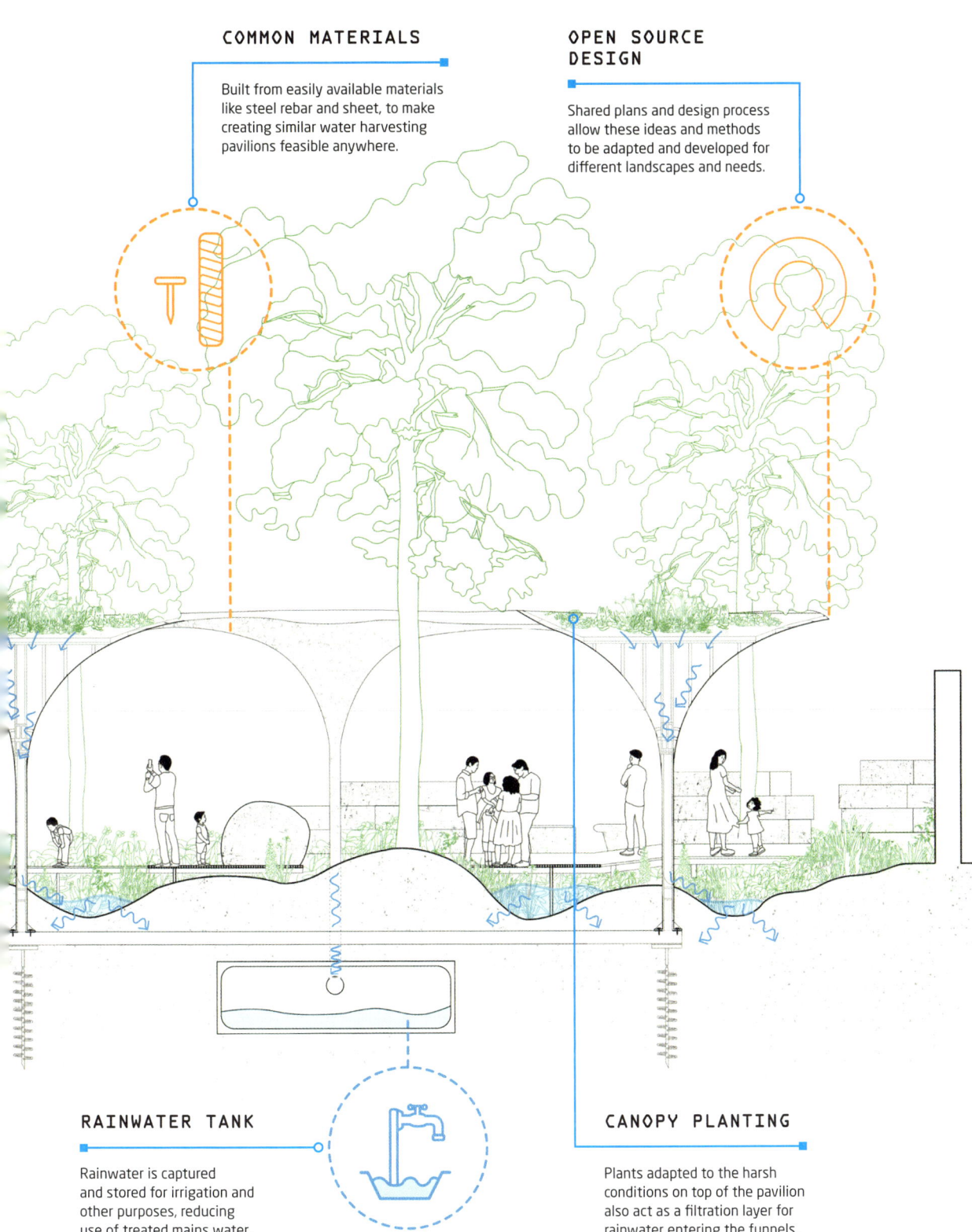

COMMON MATERIALS

Built from easily available materials like steel rebar and sheet, to make creating similar water harvesting pavilions feasible anywhere.

OPEN SOURCE DESIGN

Shared plans and design process allow these ideas and methods to be adapted and developed for different landscapes and needs.

RAINWATER TANK

Rainwater is captured and stored for irrigation and other purposes, reducing use of treated mains water.

CANOPY PLANTING

Plants adapted to the harsh conditions on top of the pavilion also act as a filtration layer for rainwater entering the funnels.

CHAPTER TWO

ACTIVE WATER HARVESTING

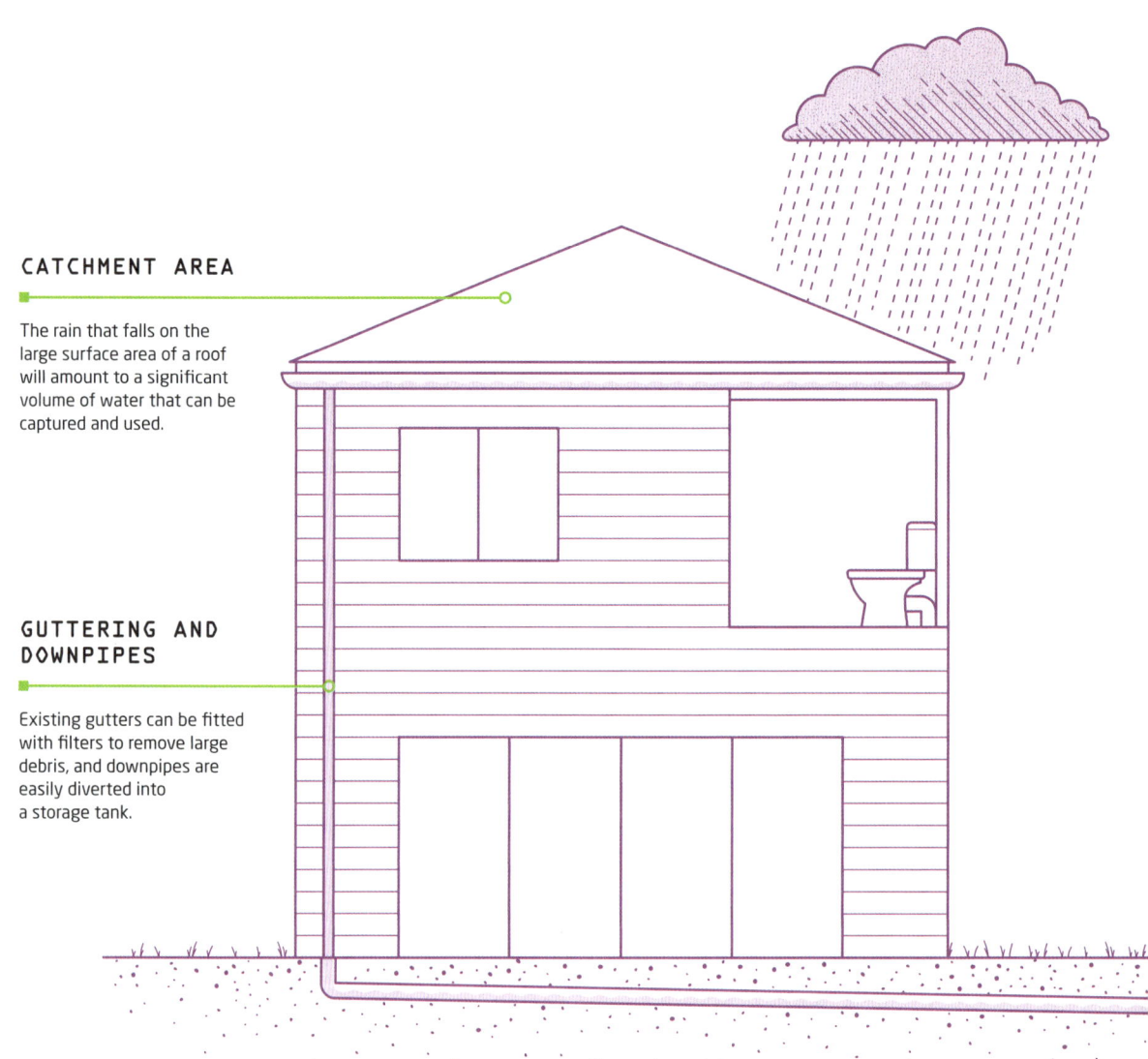

CATCHMENT AREA

The rain that falls on the large surface area of a roof will amount to a significant volume of water that can be captured and used.

GUTTERING AND DOWNPIPES

Existing gutters can be fitted with filters to remove large debris, and downpipes are easily diverted into a storage tank.

ROOFTOP RAINWATER HARVESTING

ROOFTOPS HAVE LARGE SURFACE AREAS, IDEAL FOR RAINWATER COLLECTION, AND ARE THE MOST COMMON AND WIDELY USED METHOD OF RAINWATER HARVESTING GLOBALLY. EVERY HOUSE HAS A ROOF, AND THE WATER THAT LANDS ON IT CAN AND SHOULD BE CAPTURED AND UTILIZED IN THE GARDEN OR HOME.

Domestic rainwater harvesting involves collecting and storing rainwater for later use. Once rain has fallen on a roof, gutter systems are designed to transport it away, via downpipes, which are usually connected to a drain leading to the sewer system. It is, however, straightforward to modify downpipes to flow into a rainwater harvesting tank or water butt. Gutters and downpipes can also be fitted to other structures, such as sheds or greenhouses. This water could then be used for irrigation and watering plants, non-potable purposes like flushing toilets and washing, or even for drinking if it is properly treated. Tanks and water butts should always be covered to prevent contamination, insect breeding, and algal growth.

FILTERS IN RAINWATER HARVESTING SYSTEMS

Filters are an essential addition to active rainwater harvesting systems where water is gathered and stored in tanks or water butts. They ensure that collected water is clean and suitable for its intended use, and that the system remains free of blockages. By keeping contaminants out, filters minimize the need for frequent cleaning of tanks and pumps, but need to be properly cleaned and regularly maintained themselves.

Rainwater harvesting systems typically include different stages of filtration. Gutter filters or leaf guards remove larger debris at the collection point. Inlet filters sieve out debris and sediment before water enters the tank. Fine mesh or cartridge filters can be fitted for more precise filtration, especially if water is to be used indoors. Some filters help capture organic matter, which can lead to algae or bacterial growth in the tank, while advanced setups for drinking water may include UV sterilization or reverse osmosis systems.

The filters you fit will depend on the water's intended purpose; professional advice should be sought where rainwater is harvested for household uses or drinking.

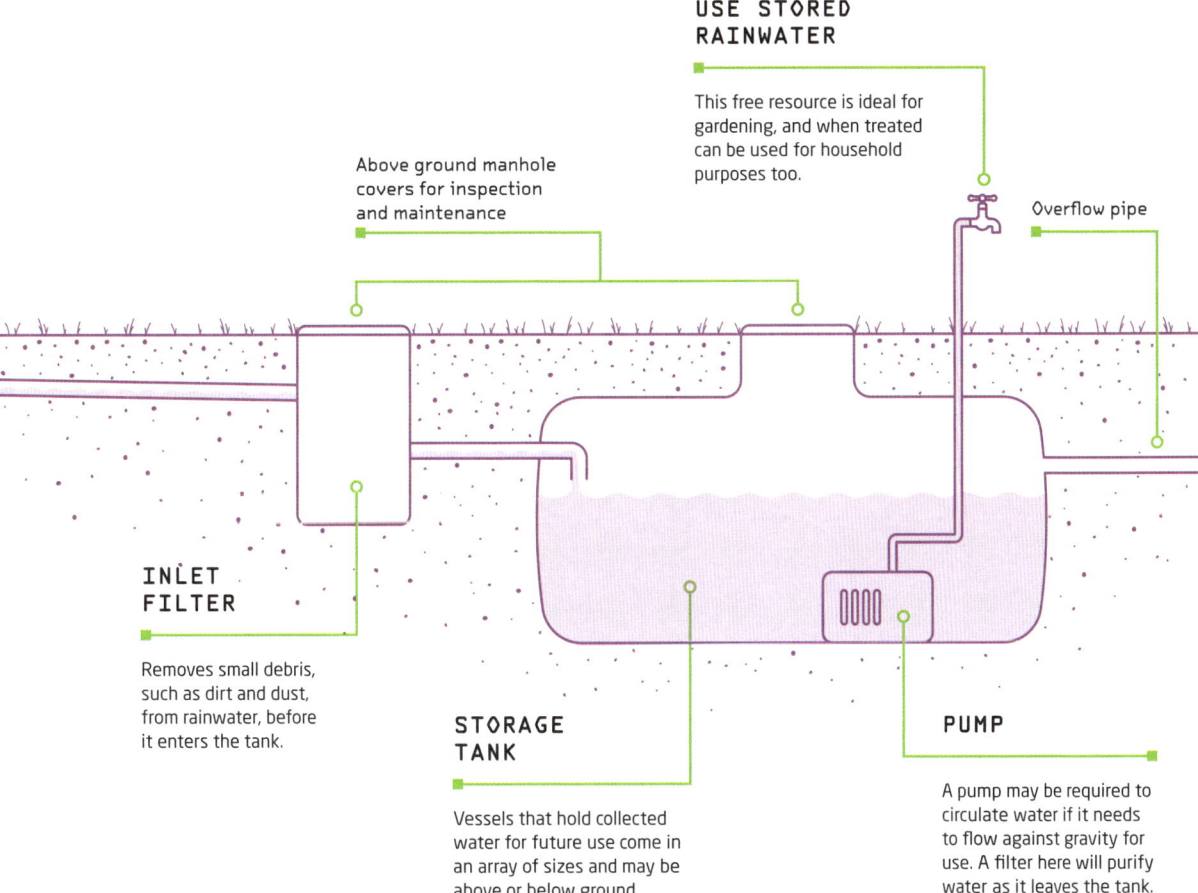

USE STORED RAINWATER
This free resource is ideal for gardening, and when treated can be used for household purposes too.

Above ground manhole covers for inspection and maintenance

Overflow pipe

INLET FILTER
Removes small debris, such as dirt and dust, from rainwater, before it enters the tank.

STORAGE TANK
Vessels that hold collected water for future use come in an array of sizes and may be above or below ground.

PUMP
A pump may be required to circulate water if it needs to flow against gravity for use. A filter here will purify water as it leaves the tank.

HOW TO STORE ROOFTOP-HARVESTED RAINWATER

CAPTURED RAINWATER NEEDS TO BE STORED READY FOR USE, AND THIS IS ESPECIALLY IMPORTANT IN AREAS THAT EXPERIENCE LONG PERIODS OF DRY WEATHER. WATER BUTTS ARE WELL SUITED TO SMALL SPACES, BUT THE EXTRA CAPACITY OF A LARGER TANK GIVES GREATER SCOPE FOR UTILIZING HARVESTED RAINWATER.

WATER BUTTS

Installing water butts creates a simple system that collects rainwater from gutters and stores it in barrels that capture water diverted from downpipes. Many different styles, types, and sizes of water butt are available, but look for examples made of recycled materials, like waste plastic, or repurposed objects, such as oak barrels, to reduce carbon impact and waste. Compact water butts can be fitted in small gardens or on balconies, as long as they can be connected to a downpipe. Some water butts also house planters on the top, which act as a filtration layer and improve the aesthetic.

CREATE A STABLE BASE

The base for a water butt or above ground tank must be stable and durable, as both are very heavy when full – water weighs 1,000kg (2,200lb) per cubic metre. Always site a butt or tank on a level surface to evenly distribute its weight. Create a solid base from sturdy materials, such as concrete (cement-free alternatives are lower carbon), paving slabs, or choose a butt or tank supplied with a purpose-built stand. The base must be large enough to fully support the bottom of the butt or tank. If in doubt, engage a professional landscaper or builder to install this for you.

Position the butt or tank at a height that allows easy access to the tap, especially for filling watering cans. Incorporate good drainage at the base to prevent pooling water eroding the foundation, or design a creative use for any overflow (see p.57).

RAINWATER DIVERTERS

Different rainwater diverter kits are available to fit various sizes and shapes of downpipes and divert the water from them into a water butt. Attaching them is a simple process.

1. Select a suitable diverter
Ensure the diverter you choose fits your downpipe size (often, but not always, 68mm/2½in round or 65mm/2½in square).

2. Position the water butt
Place the barrel on a stable, elevated base near the downpipe for easy access.

3. Install the diverter
Cut a section out of the downpipe (according to the kit instructions) using a saw and fit the diverter to the downpipe. Ensure the diverter is installed higher than the inlet to the water butt so that the water can flow downwards.

4. Connect securely
Connect the diverter to the water butt using the flexible hose supplied. Ensure watertight fittings to prevent leaks. Clear away any debris regularly.

[01] Water butts typically hold 200–500 litres (50–110 gallons), but they can be connected for greater capacity and larger sizes are available. Bespoke water butts, like this planted steel tank, can add character.
[02] Taps and hoses are installed at the bottom of the barrel for easy gravity-fed water access. Solar powered pumps can also be used for irrigation systems.

[03] Overflow systems allow excess water to be utilized or drain away when the barrel is full. A series of water butts can be connected together to collect overflow water for use.
[04] Water butts are ideal for small-scale garden applications like watering, pots, ornamental plants, and vegetable plots.

ABOVE AND BELOW GROUND STORAGE TANKS

These are large tanks placed above ground, or buried underground, to store harvested rainwater. They typically range in capacity from 1,000–20,000 litres (220–4,400 gallons), but larger and smaller sizes are also widely available. If you have the space and the budget, then go for the largest capacity possible to maximize your water storage potential. Underground tanks save space and are more discrete, but this is not always a practical option, particularly if you already have an established garden that you do not want to dig up.

> ### BELOW GROUND TANK KEY FEATURES
>
> • Hidden storage saves space and preserves the aesthetic appearance of the house and garden.
> • Tanks are generally made of plastic, so look for options manufactured from recycled materials.
> • Many tanks are supplied with an integrated water filter.
> • Pump systems are usually used to retrieve water from the tank for use - as they are below ground they cannot be gravity fed.
> • Used to supply water for garden irrigation, as well as non-potable household purposes like laundry, toilet flushing, and pressure washing.

Burying rainwater harvesting tanks underground allows these large, often unsightly containers to be hidden from view.

Surface mounted tanks are simpler to install and less costly than those below ground, but can look ugly. Their placement and screening will require planning and maintenance.

ABOVE GROUND TANK KEY FEATURES

- These tanks are usually made of plastic, metal, or concrete and require a strong, level base to support their weight when full.
- Large capacity tanks can store a significant amount of water. Modular systems are also available, allowing tanks to be connected together to further increase storage.
- Gravity-fed systems work where a tank is placed higher than the point of use, allowing gravity to distribute the water, and eliminating the need for pumps.
- Used to supply water for garden irrigation, as well as non-potable household purposes like laundry, toilet flushing, and pressure washing.

The blue-green roof on the Bloc building in Manchester, UK, uses a passive irrigation system to store rainwater that is drawn up to sustain rooftop planting.

TANKS SUPPLYING PASSIVE IRRIGATION SYSTEMS

It is possible to collect rainwater in large, shallow, underground tanks that are fed by rainwater filtering through the permeable surfaces above them, for example permeable paving (see p.88) or planted areas. They can also be fed from rooftop harvesting, if downpipes are directed to feed them. These tanks are commonly used as part of a green roof system (see opposite) or where space for other water tanks is limited. Capacity is dictated by the area a tank covers, but as they can be used structurally under paving, driveways, and hard landscaped elements, it is possible for them to be fitted beneath an entire garden. Although the rainwater in the tanks is actively collected, it is then used passively to irrigate plants through wicking systems that employ capillary action. This draws water from the tank into the dry soil above it. When this soil becomes moist, the wicking process stops, conserving water in the tank for when soil moisture falls once again.

PASSIVE IRRIGATION TANK KEY FEATURES

- Concealed water storage makes efficient use of space and does not impact the appearance of the house and garden.
- Large capacity tanks are available that can store a significant amount of water, but many sizes are available to suit a wide range of sites.
- Passive (non-pumped) system makes use of wicks to move water into dry soil via natural capillary action, keeping plants well supplied with water. No energy is required and there is no equipment to maintain.
- Used for garden irrigation.

DANGERS OF STORING RAINWATER

Rainwater storage can pose risks if not properly managed and it is important only to use stored water for the purposes intended when the system was installed. Ensuring proper filtration, regular tank maintenance, and that tanks remain covered and systems sealed, all help to mitigate any issues.

- Contamination – If not filtered and stored properly, rainwater can collect pollutants from roofs, gutters, and the air, leading to contamination.
- Mosquitoes – Water in storage tanks that are not fitted with covers can become a breeding ground for mosquitos, increasing the risk of bites and mosquito-borne diseases.
- Algal growth – Open, unsealed tanks admit sunlight, which allows algae to grow, affecting water quality.
- Waterborne diseases – Using untreated rainwater for drinking, cooking, bathing, or showering can lead to illnesses caused by pathogens, such as *E. coli*, *Legionella*, or *Giardia*.
- Structural failure – Poorly installed or maintained water tanks may leak, collapse, or cause flooding. Water is heavy, and a full tank could cause serious damage if it fails or falls.

CAPACITY OF RAINWATER HARVESTING TANKS

TOO MUCH STORAGE IS BETTER THAN TOO LITTLE, SO ONE WAY TO SELECT A TANK TO SUIT YOUR SITE AND NEEDS IS TO FIND THE LARGEST CAPACITY THAT IS AFFORDABLE AND CAN BE ACCOMMODATED UNOBTRUSIVELY. ALTERNATIVELY, MANY SUPPLIERS OFFER ONLINE CALCULATORS TO SIZE THE TANK ACCURATELY, OR USE THE FORMULA BELOW TO CALCULATE THE RIGHT CAPACITY FOR YOUR TANK.

HOW TO CALCULATE TANK CAPACITY
To determine the ideal tank capacity for your rainwater harvesting system, start by calculating how much water your roof can collect. To do this, you need to find the area of your roof and the annual rainfall in your location, which is available through local weather data services, such as the Met Office in the UK. Only include the area of the roof that feeds the downpipe or downpipes that water will be collected from. If in doubt, consult a professional water engineer for guidance.

CALCULATION
The formula below gives the amount of water that can be collected annually. Multiplying by a factor of 0.05 gives five per cent of the total rainfall that could be collected each year. This is recommended as the tank capacity by suppliers because it accounts for the fact that water will be used and the tank will be refilled by regular rainfall, ensuring efficient use of space and resources, while avoiding oversized, underutilized tanks.

Explanation
- Roof area – The surface area of your roof (length x width) in m^2. Easy to measure using Google Earth (earth.google.com).
- Drainage coefficient – Accounts for water loss due to evaporation or overflow (use 0.8 as a standard).
- Filter efficiency – Accounts for water loss during filtration (typically 0.95).
- Annual rainfall – Use local data to determine total yearly rainfall (in mm).

FORMULA FOR TANK CAPACITY

ROOF AREA (M^2) × DRAINAGE COEFFICIENT × FILTER EFFICIENCY × ANNUAL RAINFALL (MM)

× 0.05

= RECOMMENDED TANK CAPACITY (LITRES)

EXAMPLE

If average annual rainfall is 800mm (31½in) and the roof area is 100m², the formula gives a tank capacity of 3,000 litres (660 gallons).

ANNUAL RAINFALL
800MM
(31½IN)

Length 20m

Downpipe   Guttering

Width 5m

ROOF AREA
100M²

TOTAL RAINFALL
COLLECTED ANNUALLY
↓
100 × 0.8 × 0.95 × 800
=
60,800L
(13,375 GALLONS)

RECOMMENDED TANK
CAPACITY
↓
60,800 × 0.05
=
3,040L
(670 GALLONS)

A 3,000L (660 GALLON) TANK WOULD BE IDEAL IN THIS SITUATION

CALCULATING WATER USAGE

Once you know how much rainwater you can harvest, it is useful to determine exactly what this collected water will be used for and how much water is needed for these purposes. This can then be factored in when calculating the capacity of water tank required. Review recent water bills to help determine usage, and refer to records from your water meter if you have one. By considering both water collection and usage, you can design a rainwater harvesting system that efficiently conserves water and minimizes wastage. At lower ranges (150–500 litres/33–110 gallons), a water butt is sufficient, but for 500 litres (110 gallons) or more, a larger rainwater tank is a better option. Remember that it is also important to manage overflow sustainably (see opposite).

EXAMPLE GARDEN AND HOME WATER USE

- Garden use – Three 5 litre (1 gallon) watering cans daily: total usage 15 litres (3 gallons) per day. Watering with a hose or mains-fed irrigation system at 1000 litres (220 gallons) per hour for 15 minutes daily: total usage 250 litres (57 gallons) per day.

- Other potential household uses – Each laundry cycle uses about 50L (11 gallons): assume 0.25 cycles per person daily. Every toilet flush uses 5 litres (1 gallon): estimate five flushes per person daily.

FORMULA FOR TANK CAPACITY BASED ON WATER USE

Daily water usage x 365 days x 0.05 = Tank capacity (house and garden)

EXAMPLE

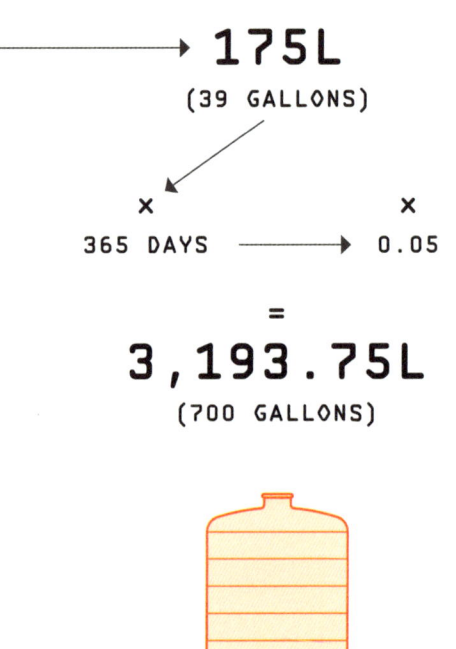

4 PEOPLE USING 40L (9 GALLONS) PER DAY
=
160L (36 GALLONS)

+

15L (3 GALLONS) OF DAILY GARDEN USE

=

175L
(39 GALLONS)
TOTAL DAILY USE

175L (39 GALLONS) x 365 DAYS x 0.05

=

3,193.75L
(700 GALLONS)

FIT A TANK WITH AT LEAST A 3,200L (700 GALLON) CAPACITY

Water that overflows from water butts or rainwater tanks can be directed into landscaped features, such as swales, rain gardens, or ephemeral ponds.

VARIABILITY IN RAINFALL

In the UK, it typically rains every three days on average throughout the year, but rainfall varies significantly with location and, wherever you live, is becoming increasingly unpredictable. If you are to rely on the rainwater you harvest for a portion of your water use it is important to take this variability in rainfall into account and plan enough storage to supply you through dry spells of weather. When sizing your tank, consider how many days' water use you want your storage to provide. Multiply the household's daily water use by the average number of dry days per month to get the total storage capacity needed.

To plan for ten dry days per month, multiply daily use by ten. For example, to supply water for garden use of 15 litres (3 gallons) per day you would need a tank with a capacity of at least 150L (33 gallons).

If you live somewhere that regularly experiences prolonged dry periods of weather, another approach to ensure that your supply of harvested rainwater will last would be to base the capacity of a tank on the most days without rainfall in the previous year in your area, multiplied by the household's average daily water use. It's really difficult to accurately calculate required capacity, because a dry period may begin when the water tank is not yet full. However, this method provides a guideline, and a safety factor can be added on top of this requirement if you have space and budget for a larger tank.

MANAGING OVERFLOW

Storage tanks are likely to overflow occasionally following prolonged periods of rain or intense storms. Sustainably managing this overflow helps use rainwater as efficiently as possible and prevent runoff causing flooding or overwhelming sewer systems (see pp.36–37). Employing passive rainwater harvesting is an ideal way to harness overflows as part of attractive garden features. Do this by directing overflow into planted areas using swales or basins (see p.85), constructing a rain garden (see p.82) with well-drained soil and water tolerant plants that will collect and filter excess water, or create soakaways – gravel-filled pits – to channel overflow into the ground.

Use rocks or splash blocks to slow water flow at discharge points and prevent soil erosion around planting areas. Utilize permeable paving (see p.88) near overflow areas to absorb water and prevent pooling or flooding. Smaller overflow tanks can also be installed to capture excess rainwater for use during dry periods. These could also be open and planted to create wildlife features.

CONDENSATE HARVESTING

An air-conditioning unit can discharge a surprising amount of water. In dry climates, an air conditioner can produce around 1 litre (1¾ pints) per day, while in humid conditions it may generate up to 68 litres (120 pints) per day. This makes the condensate produced a valuable water source for harvesting.

In this active form of water harvesting, energy input is required, but the water is a byproduct of the cooling process used in air conditioners and air source heat pumps. When warm air is cooled to reach its dew point (see box), water vapour condenses into droplets, known as "condensate", which can be collected for use.

DEW HARVESTING

This relies on the same principles as condensate harvesting (see above), but instead captures the water that condenses naturally overnight on cool surfaces to form dew. Simple structures called dew condensers have stone, metal, or plastic mesh surfaces that cool without energy input to promote dew formation, and are designed to collect the resulting water. Ancient techniques, such as stone "air wells", have long been used for this purpose.

DEW POINT

The dew point is the temperature at which the moisture content of the air becomes too great for it to be held as vapour, causing condensation to occur and dew to form. Warm air can hold more moisture, so when air cools to or below its dew point, typically at night, condensation on plants and other outdoor surfaces causes them to be covered in water droplets by early morning.

OTHER TYPES OF WATER HARVESTING

LESS COMMON WAYS TO HARVEST WATER COME INTO THEIR OWN IN DRIER REGIONS WHERE RAINFALL IS SCARCE – SOME OF THEM USING METHODS THAT HAVE EXISTED SINCE ANCIENT TIMES. THEY CAN ALSO BE USEFUL, HOWEVER, TO SUPPLEMENT STANDARD RAINWATER HARVESTING SYSTEMS.

FOG HARVESTING

Capturing water droplets from fog is valuable in fog-prone coastal or mountainous regions where rainfall is limited. Large mesh nets are installed to capture tiny water droplets from fog, which adhere to the mesh. These coalesce and drip into collection troughs for storage. It is a low-energy, low-maintenance system, but the volume of water collected varies significantly according to fog density and frequency.

SNOW HARVESTING

Snow can be collected and melted to produce water, which can be stored and used later. The snow can be gathered directly from snowfall or accumulated naturally in designated catchment areas, like fields or rooftops. This technique can be an important water source in areas with regular snowfall, especially where snow persists during dry seasons.

A fog catcher stands on a Californian hillside, its mesh screen poised to harvest condensation as clouds and mist sweep past.

SEASONAL VARIATIONS

Plants need more water in the warm spring and summer months, when they are in active growth and transpiration rates are high. During autumn and winter, when growth slows and leaves fall, transpiration rates are low and much less water is required.

PLANT SIZE AND GROWTH STAGE

No matter what its size, any plant with an established root system that is planted in the right place (see p.134) should only need watering in extreme weather. Young seedlings and anything newly planted will need regular watering (see p.62) for the establishment of new roots.

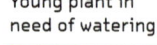
Young plant in need of watering

SOIL COMPOSITION

The texture and structure of soil affect its ability to hold water (see p.92). Dense clay soil retains moisture well, while sandy soil drains freely, which can necessitate more frequent watering. Improve moisture retention in any soil by adding an organic mulch, like compost (see pp.94–97).

LOCATION AND CONTAINER PLANTS

Root-restricted or rain-shadowed plants, such as those planted near walls, often experience dry conditions and may need watering. Plants in containers can only access the water in the pot, so will need regular watering. Position plants carefully to mitigate these issues.

SUSTAINABLE WATERING

UNDERSTANDING THE NEEDS OF PLANTS AND IMPLEMENTING EFFICIENT WATERING PRACTICES WILL ALLOW YOU TO CULTIVATE A THRIVING GARDEN WHILE CONSERVING WATER SUPPLIES. STORED RAINWATER IS IDEAL FOR GARDEN USE, AND IS A FREE AND SUSTAINABLE RESOURCE FOR GARDENERS.

Gardeners are often advised to keep plants "well-watered", but generalizing in this way is not helpful, because each plant has unique needs. Container plants in sunny conditions, for instance, may require daily watering, as might new plantings in warmer weather, while established plants should only need additional watering during severe drought.

When planted in suitable conditions (see p.134), most plants are more resilient than we might expect, and will survive with little or no watering. Lawns, for example, don't die during hot summer weather, but go brown and dormant, turning green again once rain falls (see p.145). Gardening sustainably in a changing climate will require us to change our preconceptions of gardens and landscapes, and move away from lush, green verdancy being the only acceptable aesthetic.

SIGNS OF UNDER-WATERING

- Stunted growth or lack of flowers and fruit.
- Dull or discoloured leaves.
- Leaves browning, curling, or dropping.
- Wilting plants (may also indicate overwatering).
- Lightweight pots for potted or indoor plants.
- Symptoms of powdery mildew (white, dusty leaves) indicating stress.

EFFECTIVE WATERING TECHNIQUES

IN ORDER TO MAKE EFFICIENT USE OF WATER SUPPLIES AND PROVIDE MAXIMUM BENEFIT TO PLANTS, WATER NEEDS TO REACH THE SOIL AROUND THEIR ROOTS. ALWAYS TEST SOIL MOISTURE FIRST TO SEE IF WATERING IS NECESSARY AND APPLY WATER DIRECTLY TO THE SOIL RATHER THAN TO THE LEAVES.

HOW MUCH AND HOW OFTEN TO WATER

The amount of water needed depends on a plant's requirements, the soil type, and the weather conditions. Plants growing in containers, or anywhere where their roots are restricted, will need more frequent watering, since they draw moisture from a smaller volume of soil. A good rule of thumb for container plants is to apply 10 per cent of the container's volume with each watering, so a 10 litre (2 gallon) pot would receive 1 litre (1¾ pints) of water. Daily watering may be needed during hot summer weather, but it's always best to test the compost moisture regularly.

Plants growing in open soil need watering much less frequently; usually only in very hot, dry spells of weather. Avoid light watering that only moistens the soil surface. It is always more beneficial to water thoroughly but less frequently, to ensure that moisture penetrates into the soil and reaches the depths where roots grow. This encourages deeper rooting, which also allows plants to exploit all of the naturally available soil moisture. Generally, free-draining sandy soils require more frequent but smaller amounts of water, while heavier clay soils are better given larger, less frequent applications.

WATERING METHODS

Watering cans Simple and effective, these allow targeted delivery of rainwater at the base of plants, but are labour intensive.

Hosepipes Easy to use, with attachments to direct water flow. Need pressure so often fitted to a mains tap. Wasteful if used carelessly.

Active irrigation Convenient once installed. Delivers rainwater directly to the base of plants via leaky pipes, drip nozzles, or small sprinklers. Light watering can promote shallow rooting, and inefficient timers will activate the system regardless of need.

Sprinkler systems Usually use mains water, which is sprayed into the air, where more is lost to evaporation and drifts on any wind. Best avoided.

Passive irrigation Rainwater tanks beneath lawns or planting areas (see p.53), or reservoirs at the base of pots, use wicking systems to irrigate soil without any energy input.

A hosepipe fed from a mains tap is an inefficient and wasteful way to water your garden, which should be avoided, especially for unnecessary lawn irrigation.

RAINWATER STORAGE

A rainwater tank must be raised to provide water pressure and be fitted with an inlet filter to remove debris that could clog pipes and drip nozzles.

TIMER

Adding a timer allows irrigation to be automated, with water flow switched on and off at times scheduled to suit your plants.

AUTOMATED DRIP IRRIGATION SYSTEMS

Active drip irrigation systems use long hose-like pipes fitted with small nozzles to deliver water directly to the soil above plant roots. They can efficiently manage watering in larger areas, but need to be set up carefully to avoid wastage and should always use harvested rainwater rather than mains water. Ensure the water tank is raised to provide the system with some gravity-fed water pressure. While automated systems fitted with programmable timers offer many advantages, such as efficiency and convenience, they also come with downsides, including cost, the need for regular maintenance, and the potential to waste water if not managed during cooler or wetter weather.

PROS OF AUTOMATED DRIP IRRIGATION

EFFICIENT Delivers water directly to soil near plant roots, reducing water wastage through evaporation and runoff, and helping to maintain optimal moisture levels.

SUSTAINABLE If fed from rainwater harvesting tanks where suitable filters have been fitted.

LABOUR-SAVING Programmable systems can operate on your chosen schedule, freeing up time.

CONSISTENT Provide regular watering, which can produce healthier plants and increase crop yields.

ADAPTABLE Smart systems can adjust watering schedules based on weather conditions and soil moisture levels (see box).

CONS OF AUTOMATED DRIP IRRIGATION

INITIAL COST The setup cost can be high, with expenses for equipment, installation, and maintenance.

OPERATING AND TROUBLESHOOTING Automated systems can be complicated and time consuming to get working correctly.

DEPENDENCE ON TECHNOLOGY Malfunctions or system failures can lead to over- or under-watering. Relying on automation reduces plant health monitoring.

MAINTENANCE Regular maintenance, including checking for leaks, clogs, and ensuring sensors are working, is necessary to keep the system functioning properly.

MANAGEMENT Water needs change through the year, so timers and flow need to be adjusted to deliver what's needed and prevent waste.

MATERIALS Pipes, nozzles, and other components are usually made of plastic.

SMART RAINWATER HARVESTING SYSTEMS

Smart rainwater harvesting systems use soil moisture sensors and data from weather forecasts to monitor and manage rainwater collection, storage, and release. Controlled by AI (artificial intelligence), they adjust water output by responding to soil conditions and upcoming rainfall, improving efficiency and preventing overwatering and flooding. AI has other promising applications for water conservation, including predictive analytics that identify leaks in utility networks, and powerful modelling to optimize water treatment facilities and help improve drought forecasting. These benefits, however, must be balanced with the fact that AI data centres need vast volumes of water for cooling.

MAIN LINE

A length of pipe, usually made from plastic, links to the tap and carries water from the tank to the planted area.

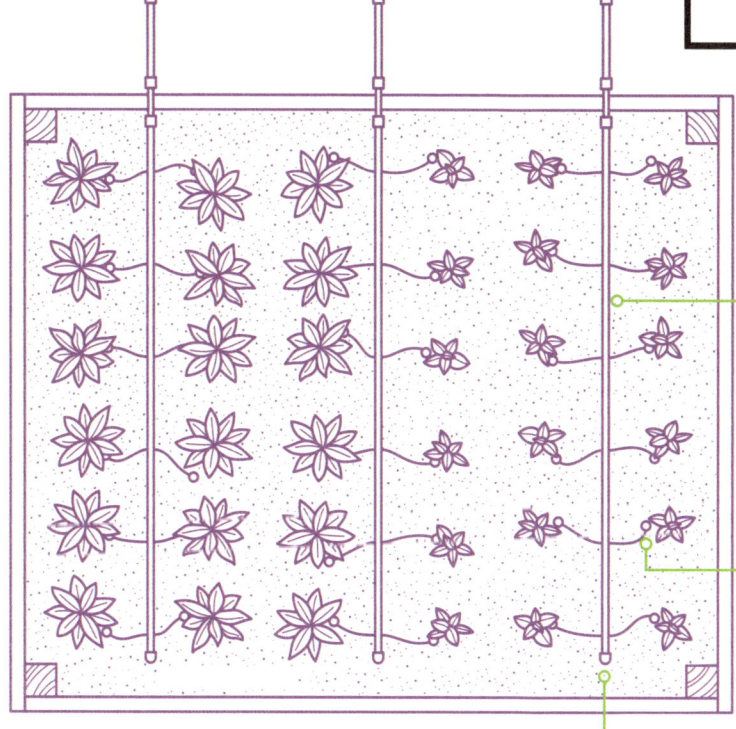

DRIP LINE

Fitted at intervals with small nozzles that drip feed water, this pipe is laid on the soil to deliver water where it is needed. Leaky or perforated pipes can also be used.

Drip nozzle

Stop end

SUITABLE FOR

Plants in soil

Plants in pots

Greenhouses

Polytunnels

Allotments

WHEN IS THE BEST TIME TO WATER?

WHEN SHOULD YOU WATER PLANTS TO MAXIMIZE THE BENEFITS AND MINIMIZE WATER LOSS? EVENING OR MORNING, MIDDAY OR MIDNIGHT? I'VE ASKED TWO EXPERTS WHAT TIME OF DAY THEY WATER THEIR OWN GARDENS TO TRY AND FIND THE ANSWER.

In a discussion with Professor Alistair Griffiths (RHS Director of Science and Collections) and Dr Mark Gush (RHS Head of Environmental Horticulture) the two agreed that it's best to avoid watering during the heat of the day. However, they choose to water their own gardens at different times that best suit the conditions in each.

Alistair's view was that watering in the evening is better, because when the sun is low and the temperature is cooler, less water will be lost from soil through evaporation and moisture will percolate into the soil more effectively. Mark didn't disagree with these points, but favours watering in the early morning. This is because he finds that night watering attracts slugs and snails, which cause unwanted damage to his plants.

My view is that midday is obviously not ideal: on sunny days it will be too hot and may risk potential leaf scorch to certain types of plants (see box). Midnight for most people will be impractical. I personally enjoy watering my garden at the end of the day, when I find it relaxing and a nice way to switch from work to rest mode.

It's useful to note that water uptake by roots is driven by water loss (transpiration) from the leaves, which occurs during daylight hours when photosynthesis is taking place and leaf pores (stomata) are open. Evening watering allows time for water to soak into the soil around the plants' root systems, and will ensure that the roots can access plenty of moisture if it's going to be hot the next day. Watering early in the morning can be just as good, but if it's going to be an especially hot day, or your plants are very exposed, this might not allow time for sufficient water to be absorbed before it evaporates. Soil type also influences the speed that water infiltrates into soil (see pp.92–93).

MYTH BUSTING – DOES WATERING DURING THE DAY CAUSE SCORCHED LEAVES?

Are you risking scorching your plants leaves by watering them during the day? In most cases, probably not. Scorching is caused by a round water droplet sitting on a leaf long enough for it to focus sunlight, like a magnifying glass effect, and burn the foliage. Most leaves have evolved to shed water, so droplets run off before this becomes a problem. Some plants are at higher risk, such as those with hairy leaves that tend to hold water, or succulents that keep water in droplets on foliage. Generally it's best practice not to water at midday, but an occasional watering, aiming at the base of the plants and away from foliage, is probably going to be fine.

PLANT WATER UPTAKE AND LOSS OVER 24 HOURS

When deciding when to water plants, consider three factors: at which time of day water uptake from roots is highest, when most water is lost from leaves, and the period when soil water evaporation is highest. These all peak in the daytime heat, suggesting it is indeed best to water in the morning or late evening.

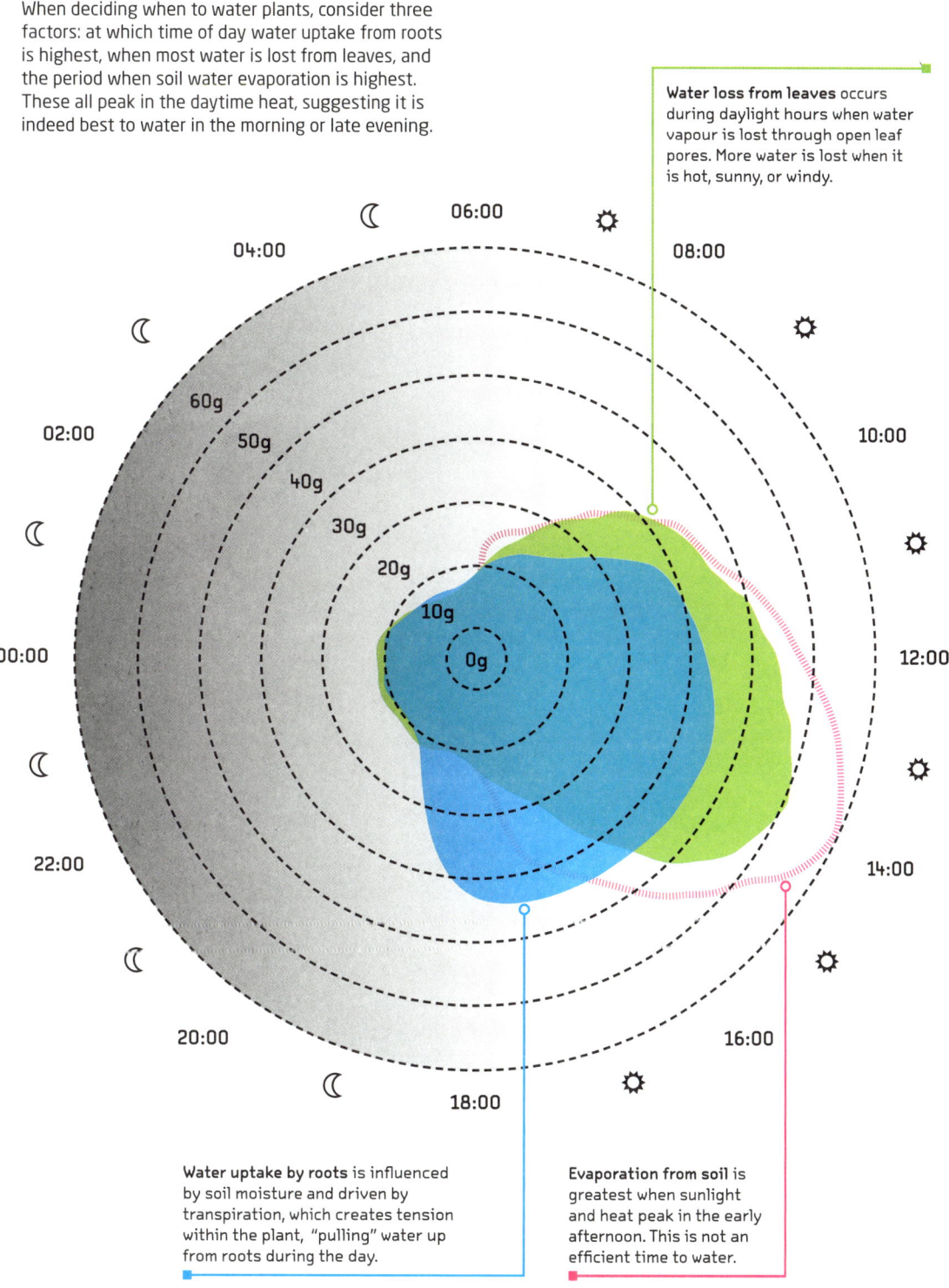

Water loss from leaves occurs during daylight hours when water vapour is lost through open leaf pores. More water is lost when it is hot, sunny, or windy.

Water uptake by roots is influenced by soil moisture and driven by transpiration, which creates tension within the plant, "pulling" water up from roots during the day.

Evaporation from soil is greatest when sunlight and heat peak in the early afternoon. This is not an efficient time to water.

ACTIVE WATER HARVESTING

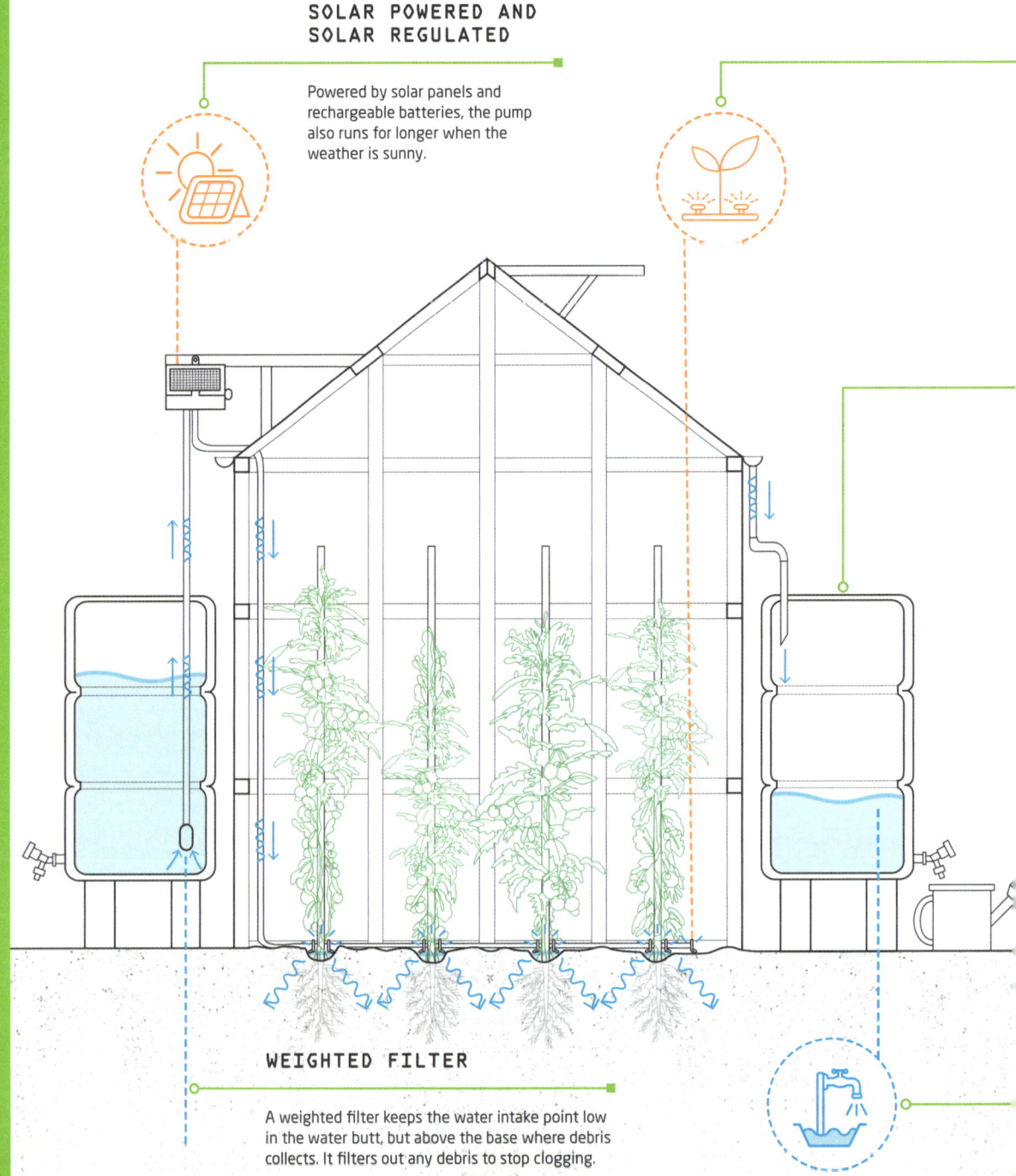

SOLAR POWERED AND SOLAR REGULATED

Powered by solar panels and rechargeable batteries, the pump also runs for longer when the weather is sunny.

WEIGHTED FILTER

A weighted filter keeps the water intake point low in the water butt, but above the base where debris collects. It filters out any debris to stop clogging.

SOLAR POWERED IRRIGATION SYSTEM This system, set up by Dr Mark Gush on his allotment, uses low-cost, innovative technology to water glasshouse plants efficiently using harvested rainwater. The system draws from a water butt that collects rainwater from a nearby shed roof.

DRIP IRRIGATION AT THE ROOTS

Nozzles positioned at the base of each plant ensure water is delivered directly to roots, which is efficient and improves plant health.

COVER WATER BUTT TO PREVENT CONTAMINATION

A lid helps stop debris and algae building up in the water butt. It also blocks the entry of slugs, snails, and other creatures that might drown.

RAINWATER HARVESTING FOR IRRIGATION

Adding a tap allows the collected rainwater to be used to water other areas of the allotment, further reducing use of mains water.

CASE STUDY

> "FREQUENT VISITS TO WATER THE ALLOTMENT ARE NO LONGER NECESSARY, WHICH IS ESPECIALLY USEFUL FOR GLASSHOUSE PLANTS WITH NO ACCESS TO RAINFALL."
>
> **DR MARK GUSH**

The system's pump is powered by a small solar panel and rechargeable batteries, and is triggered automatically by a timer, to feed a drip irrigation system with a nozzle at the base of each plant. This means frequent visits to water the allotment are no longer necessary, which is especially useful for glasshouse plants with no access to rainfall.

A further advantage is that the system automatically regulates water supply relative to the transpirational (water uptake) demand of the plants. The solar panel not only supplies power, but is also responsive to levels of solar radiation, enabling the system to provide more water when conditions are sunny (consequently hot within a glasshouse), and less water when it is heavily overcast or rainy (so cooler in a glasshouse). I create shallow, concave depressions around the base of each plant to concentrate the water that is applied where it is most needed. There are also five settings on the controller that can be used to increase or decrease applications of water.

SIMPLE TO INSTALL AND MAINTAIN

This system was relatively simple to set up. The controller, which houses the solar panels, is mounted in an unshaded, south-facing position on a piece of timber attached to the glasshouse. A water butt that collects rainwater provides the water source, and water is extracted via an intake pipe, which is fitted with a filter to prevent debris clogging the pipes and nozzles. The layout for the intake pipe, dripper lines, and dripper outlets, should be pre-planned within the constraints of the pipe lengths supplied.

Maintenance involves checking that there is sufficient water in the water butt (a low water level indicator is supplied with the system), and that the dripper nozzles are not blocked by debris or spider webs. Remove and store the controller and batteries in winter (if the system is not in use), and clean any debris from the drippers and water butt.

UNDERSTANDING AND USING GREY WATER

GREY WATER IS WASTE WATER FROM BATHS, SHOWERS, SINKS, AND OTHER DOMESTIC SOURCES THAT DOES NOT CONTAIN SEWAGE. IT CAN BE A VALUABLE RESOURCE, PARTICULARLY DURING DROUGHT, WHEN MAINS WATER USE IS RESTRICTED AND SUPPLIES OF COLLECTED RAINWATER ARE LOW.

COLLECTING AND STORING GREY WATER

The best sources of grey water are baths, showers, and sink-based dish washing, because they are easy to collect and don't contain the strong detergents and salts used in washing machines and dishwashers, which can build up in soil and be harmful to plants (see opposite). Bath and shower water can simply be collected using a bucket or similar container – place it in the shower to catch surplus water, or use a plug to retain water if you have a shower fitted over a bath. Using a plastic washing up bowl that fits into your sink means that grey water can be lifted and carried outside once the dishes are clean.

There is no need to filter grey water for outdoor use, because small organic particles, like food or hair, will break down naturally on the soil. However, this contamination means that it is important to use grey water promptly – within 24 hours of collection – to prevent bacteria breeding and any unpleasant odours. Storing untreated grey water in tanks is not recommended and it should not be allowed to contaminate tanks or butts used to store rainwater. However, rainwater can be used to dilute or supplement grey water if it is mixed in a separate container, such as a watering can, then used promptly for irrigation.

Bathwater can easily be siphoned into a container placed outside by feeding a length of pipe through an open window.

Dish washing water can be used in the garden directly from a washing up bowl.

USING GREY WATER IN THE GARDEN

While rainwater is always the first choice for garden use, grey water can be a useful short-term alternative, especially during dry spells. It is suitable for watering lawns, trees, and ornamental plants, but should not be used on edible crops due to the risk of microbial contamination. Unfiltered grey water is best applied with a watering can, as grease and particles will clog irrigation systems.

Soil and compost can filter out some contaminants, such as soap and detergents, and some residues may even act as a mild fertilizer for plants. However, studies on garden use of grey water carried out by scientists at the RHS concluded that without filtration it can be useful during water shortages, but should be used with caution.

Their experiments showed that applying grey water for several weeks did not harm most plants, though some, including *Stachys byzantina*, showed signs of salt stress after six weeks and benefitted from a rinse with rainwater. One of the main threats to plant health is boron in detergents; choosing potassium-based soaps reduces the risk of damage.

With Cranfield University, the RHS is supporting research to develop domestic-scale plant-based systems to clean grey water, making it suitable for general use, as an alternative to expensive filter systems.

CHAPTER THREE

PASSIVE RAINWATER HARVESTING

COLLECTING AND MANAGING RAINWATER NATURALLY

PASSIVE RAINWATER HARVESTING CAPTURES RAINWATER USING GRAVITY, WITHOUT MECHANICAL SYSTEMS OR HUMAN-MADE STORAGE TANKS. IT OFTEN RELIES ON SIMPLE EARTHWORKS, SUCH AS BERMS OR SWALES, TO DIRECT WATER FLOW, CREATING MOISTURE-RETENTIVE AREAS THAT BENEFIT PLANTS, WHILE HELPING TO PREVENT RUNOFF AND FLOODING.

Unlike active systems, which store rainwater in tanks and require active inputs to release that water, passive harvesting directs rainwater that falls on roofs and other collection surfaces so that it can benefit the landscape. When rainwater is absorbed into the soil, rather than running off the surface, the process is known as "infiltration". Crucial in passive rainwater harvesting, infiltration allows water to penetrate into the ground, making it available to plants without the need for time-consuming watering.

Redirecting your downpipes to channel rainwater into carefully designed landscape interventions not only reduces stormwater runoff, but also transforms your garden into a vibrant space with opportunities to include a diverse range of plants and attract wildlife. This approach enhances biodiversity, improves soil health, and creates an attractive, sustainable outdoor area for you to enjoy.

Earthworks, such as berms, swales, and ephemeral ponds (see pp.84–87), create channels and undulations that guide rainwater into the soil and areas of planting. This approach supports plant growth and replenishes groundwater, while reducing runoff after heavy rain, soil erosion, and the risk of flooding. Passive systems can be employed to manage overflow from the rainwater harvesting tanks and water butts used in active water harvesting systems (see p.57).

WATER AS HABITAT

Wetlands are important wildlife habitats that are being lost due to development, pollution, and climate change. Using passive water harvesting to create wetland habitats in your garden, whether a rain garden, ephemeral pond, or swale, is a great way to boost biodiversity and support local populations of wildlife.

[01] Wetlands are full of biodiversity; this species-rich wetland meadow, including common spotted orchid (*Dactylorhiza fuchsii*), can be recreated in moist garden soil.
[02] By improving infiltration, passive systems support plant growth, maintain soil health, and help to protect against flooding.
[03] Directing runoff into planted areas, contouring land to guide rainwater, and applying mulch can all promote rainwater infiltration.

RECHARGING AQUIFERS

Aquifers are formed where areas of porous rock hold groundwater, creating a resource that is vital for providing drinking water and sustaining ecosystems. Using permeable surfaces allows water to infiltrate into the soil and replenish aquifers. This helps to ensure a sustainable water supply, prevent ground subsidence, and protect against saltwater intrusion in coastal areas.

[Above] Urban areas with high proportions of impermeable surfaces, such as tarmac roads, are prone to flooding because water cannot infiltrate into the ground.
[Left] Permeable surfaces, like those used in my Yard House design, help to mitigate flooding. Here gravel-filled, planted channels separate slabs laid on a permeable sub-base.

THE IMPORTANCE OF PERMEABLE SURFACES

INCORPORATING PERMEABLE SURFACES INTO LANDSCAPES AND GARDENS IS KEY TO PASSIVE WATER HARVESTING AND PREVENTING RUNOFF. DESIGNERS MAKE USE OF PERMEABLE SURFACES, RAIN GARDENS, AND SWALES TO CREATE SUSTAINABLE DRAINAGE SYSTEMS (SUDS) THAT MANAGE RAINWATER WHERE IT FALLS.

PROBLEMS CAUSED BY IMPERMEABILITY

Impermeable surfaces, like paving laid on a mortar bed, concrete, asphalt, and rooftops, are everywhere in urban landscapes and around our homes. They prevent water infiltration, causing it to flow quickly across the surface during heavy rain. This runoff is called stormwater and is an increasing problem as climate change causes more intense rainfall events (see p.20). Large volumes of stormwater can overwhelm drainage and sewer systems (see p.36), leading to urban flooding, soil erosion, and water pollution. Flash flooding is much more likely when heavily urbanized areas have a high percentage of impermeable surfaces.

THE BENEFITS OF PERMEABLE SURFACES

Many surfaces are permeable to water, including planted areas, lawns, gravel, and permeable paving (see p.88). These are valuable because they allow rainwater to infiltrate into the ground where it falls, slowing water flow and reducing runoff, which in turn reduces the load on drainage systems and the risk of flooding. Permeable surfaces also promote natural processes, such as recharging groundwater (see box), and help to filter out pollutants before they reach waterways or aquifers.

WHAT ARE SUDS?

Implementing Sustainable Drainage Systems (SuDS) creates attractive landscapes while managing stormwater effectively, by mimicking natural drainage processes. Varied strategies, such as permeable paving (see p.88), green roofs (see p.89), swales (see p.85), and rain gardens (see p.82) are used to slow the flow of rainwater, allowing it to infiltrate into the ground. This helps to prevent flooding, reduces the need for irrigation, improves water quality, and promotes the recharging of groundwater.

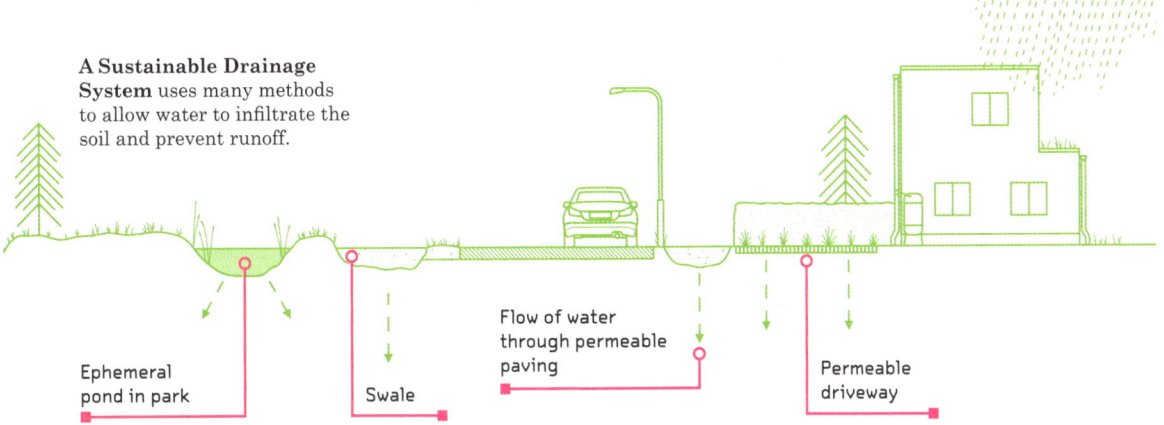

A Sustainable Drainage System uses many methods to allow water to infiltrate the soil and prevent runoff.

- Ephemeral pond in park
- Swale
- Flow of water through permeable paving
- Permeable driveway

PASSIVE RAINWATER HARVESTING

CASE STUDY

SHEFFIELD CITY COUNCIL'S GREY TO GREEN PROJECT, with planting design led by Professor Nigel Dunnett of Sheffield University, has transformed what was a concrete-heavy cityscape into a sustainable, biodiverse green corridor.

[Far left] Sheffield Grey to Green's vibrant seasonal planting, incorporating flowering perennials and trees well adapted to the street-side conditions, has transformed this area of the city.
[Left] Barrier dams built into these sloped planting areas help to manage water flow during heavy rainfall.

This green initiative in the heart of Sheffield integrates Sustainable Drainage Systems (SuDS) (see p.77) with large, vibrantly planted areas, to address issues such as flooding, biodiversity loss, and urban cooling. It is also designed to create safe, attractive spaces that encourage residents to walk and cycle, and provides a model for the use of nature-based solutions in public spaces.

SUSTAINABLE WATER MANAGEMENT STRATEGIES

At the heart of Grey to Green is its innovative water management. Design guidance was provided by Kevin Barton of Robert Bray Associates to create SuDS to slow, capture, and infiltrate rainwater to prevent surface flooding. The key features include planted swales (see p.85), permeable surfaces (see p.88), and carefully engineered soils that optimize water infiltration and retention. These mimic natural hydrological processes, reducing reliance on conventional drainage systems and ensuring the resilience of plants during extreme weather events.

The project's success hinges on its carefully engineered soil, or substrate, created by blending recycled compost and glass with crushed sandstone and a small amount of loam, which enables runoff water from impermeable roadways to infiltrate into planted areas and provides moisture for plant growth. It is planted with a varied selection of perennial plant species, and topped with crushed sandstone mulch. This dual functionality – balancing permeability and water retention – creates ideal conditions for robust, low-maintenance planting that requires no additional irrigation. Without such innovation, SuDS would struggle to achieve their full potential, highlighting the importance of soils in waterwise design.

BALANCING FUNCTIONALITY AND BEAUTY

Plant selection is another cornerstone of the project. Species were chosen for their abilities to cope with the varying moisture levels across the site, ensuring their survival during droughts or heavy rainfall. A mix of plants – some drought tolerant, some flood-resilient, and some adapted to thrive in both conditions – reduce maintenance demands, while offering year-round visual interest through diverse textures and colours.

This thoughtful selection includes both native and non-native plant species. Native plants support local wildlife, but non-natives can also provide useful habitat and food resources, while adding resilience to the planting and extending flowering periods. Together, they increase biodiversity by creating habitats that attract pollinators and other species. Additionally, the green spaces contribute to urban cooling and filter pollutants, which improves air quality, providing a healthier environment.

RESILIENT PLANTS FROM THE SWALES

- *Achillea* 'Coronation Gold'
- *Calamagrostis* x *acutiflora* 'Karl Foerster'
- *Carex secta*
- *Eremurus* x *isabellinus* 'Cleopatra'
- *Kniphofia triangularis*
- *Oenothera lindheimeri* (syn. *Gaura lindheimeri*)
- *Rudbeckia fulgida* var. *deamii*
- *Salvia nemorosa* 'Caradonna'
- *Sisyrinchium striatum*

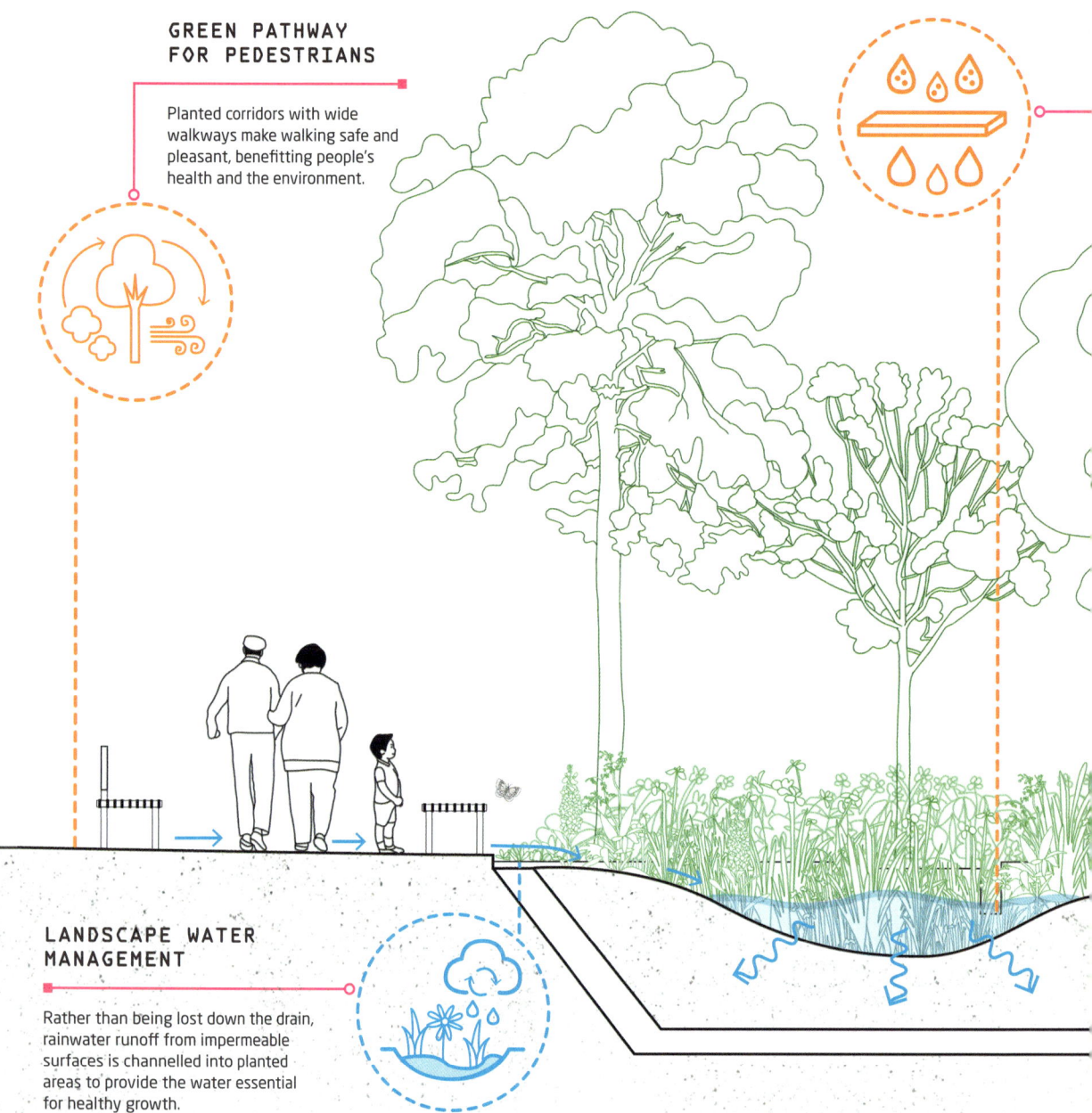

GREEN PATHWAY FOR PEDESTRIANS

Planted corridors with wide walkways make walking safe and pleasant, benefitting people's health and the environment.

LANDSCAPE WATER MANAGEMENT

Rather than being lost down the drain, rainwater runoff from impermeable surfaces is channelled into planted areas to provide the water essential for healthy growth.

LONG-TERM SUCCESS THROUGH AFTERCARE

Ongoing care has been crucial to maintaining the project's impact. Regular monitoring ensures that plants flourish and that SuDS function effectively. Challenges such as weed control, plant overgrowth, and system upkeep are addressed through scheduled maintenance. By engaging local councils and communities in these efforts, the project has fostered shared responsibility and secured its long-term success.

BROADER IMPACTS

The Grey to Green project has transformed this part of Sheffield's urban landscape into a biodiverse, sustainable environment, offering significant ecological, social, and aesthetic benefits. It demonstrates how urban areas can effectively manage water, enhance biodiversity, and combat urban heat islands while creating visually compelling public spaces.

This innovative initiative serves as an inspiration for other cities, showcasing how thoughtful design and collaboration can address environmental challenges and improve urban living. As urban populations grow and climate challenges intensify, projects like Grey to Green illustrate how it is possible for cities to be greener and more sustainable.

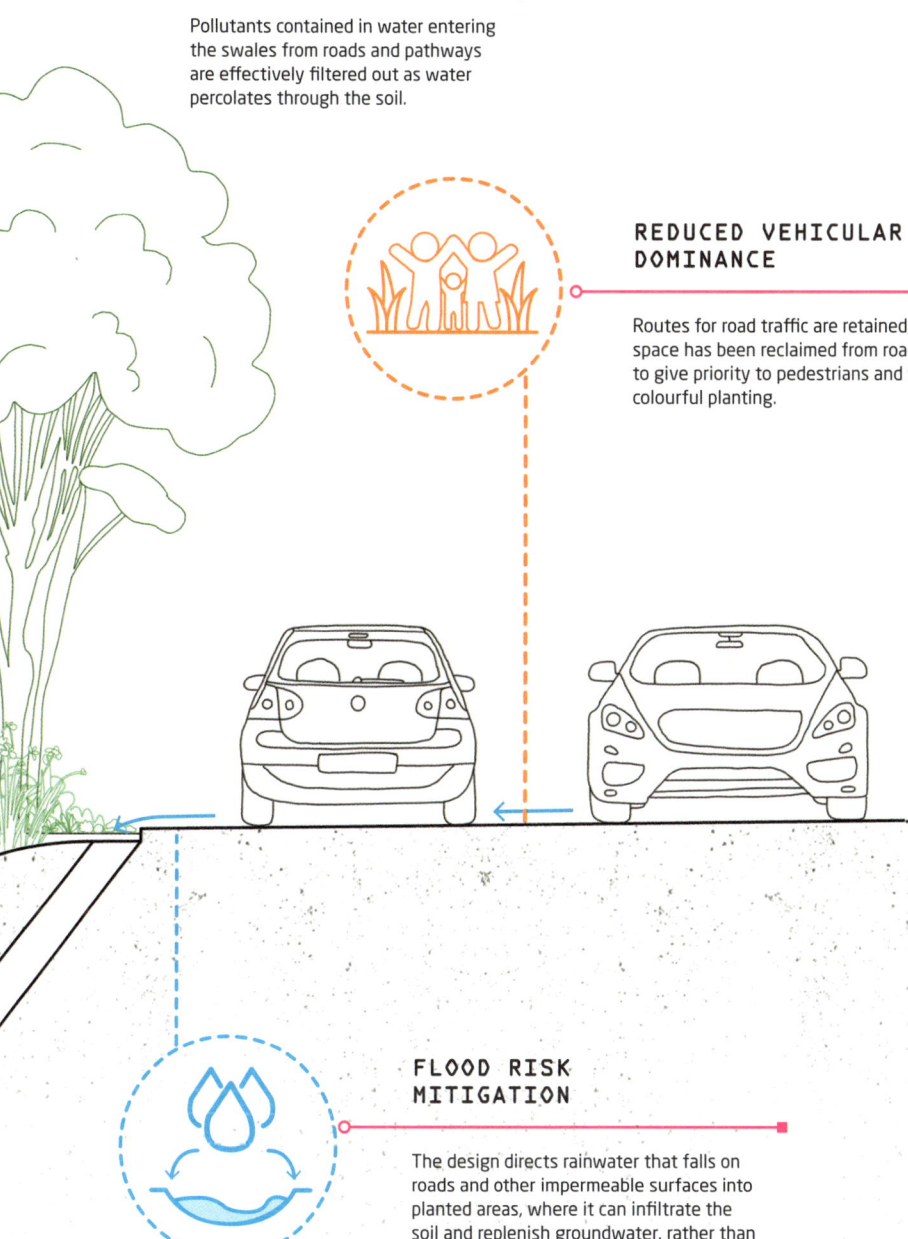

SWALES FILTER RAINWATER RUNOFF

Pollutants contained in water entering the swales from roads and pathways are effectively filtered out as water percolates through the soil.

REDUCED VEHICULAR DOMINANCE

Routes for road traffic are retained, but space has been reclaimed from roadways to give priority to pedestrians and varied, colourful planting.

FLOOD RISK MITIGATION

The design directs rainwater that falls on roads and other impermeable surfaces into planted areas, where it can infiltrate the soil and replenish groundwater, rather than overloading storm drains and mains sewers.

"GREY TO GREEN DEMONSTRATES HOW URBAN AREAS CAN EFFECTIVELY MANAGE WATER, ENHANCE BIODIVERSITY, AND COMBAT URBAN HEAT ISLANDS WHILE CREATING VISUALLY COMPELLING PUBLIC SPACES."

RAIN GARDENS

A RAIN GARDEN IS A PLANTED AREA THAT CAPTURES AND ABSORBS RAINWATER RUNOFF FROM IMPERMEABLE SURFACES LIKE ROOFS, DRIVEWAYS, AND STREETS. RAIN GARDENS HELP TO REDUCE FLOODING AND IMPROVE WATER QUALITY, AND ALSO PROMOTE BIODIVERSITY BY PROVIDING FOOD, WATER, AND HABITATS FOR WILDLIFE.

These gardens typically feature a dip or depression in the ground that receives rainwater runoff from impermeable surfaces that lie at a higher level. Rainwater is often channelled into the garden via a redirected downpipe from the roof of a house, garage, or shed. They also make a useful outlet for any overflow from water butts and tanks (see p.57). Water collects in the garden's depression, but is allowed to drain away naturally, which creates growing conditions for plants that vary according to both the amount of rainfall and the location within the design. Rain gardens are not intended to hold water for more than 48 hours, to prevent stagnant standing water. This means that plants need to be chosen carefully (see Plant Directory pp.146–181), some to grow well in permanently moist conditions, but most to cope with a changing environment where soil may be either wet or dry.

NATURAL WATER MANAGEMENT
The aggregates, soil, and plants that make up a rain garden retain and filter stormwater, allowing it to infiltrate into the ground, rather than flow into storm drains and on into sewer systems. Filtering water through layers of soil and plant roots in this way improves water quality by trapping pollutants, such as heavy metals and chemical fertilizers. Rain gardens are an effective tool for sustainable landscaping and urban water management, because they can reduce flooding and drainage problems without the need for expensive drainage systems. If well designed, rain gardens require little maintenance once established.

RAIN GARDEN BENEFITS

- Minimal maintenance required – no need for watering once plants are established.
- Absorbs up to 30 per cent more water than a standard lawn.
- Provides a diverse planting area for a range of plant species.
- Slows heavy rainfall, reducing soil erosion.
- Attracts beneficial wildlife, like insects and birds.
- Can remove the need to install a soakaway system (see p.87) by naturally managing runoff, infiltrating water, and recharging ground water supplies.
- Keeps water out of mains sewer systems, preventing potential water pollution (see pp.36-37).

[Above] Bridget Joyce Square Community Rain Park, by Robert Bray Associates, captures runoff from the surrounding hardscape and channels it into a sunken planted area.
[Right] Thinking creatively about how to supply a rain garden allowed designer Nicola Haines to make an interesting feature from weathered steel rainwater channels.

Earthworks not only add visual interest to a garden or landscape, but are also essential components of passive water harvesting techniques, which enable rainwater to be managed and utilized effectively. They are used to form mounds, depressions, and channels to direct and slow water flow, and create areas where water can infiltrate soil, reducing runoff. Berms, swales, recharge trenches, soakaways, infiltration basins, and ephemeral ponds are all land formations created to manage water flow, prevent soil erosion, and allow water to infiltrate into the soil and recharge groundwater supplies. These different earthworks can all be incorporated into a rain garden (see p.82) or be used to manage overflow from a rain garden or water storage tank (see p.57).

BERMS

Raised mounds of soil, or berms, are used to divert water to specific areas, such as rain gardens or ponds (see p.86). They are often made using soil excavated to form other features, such as ponds, or swales. The barrier they create allows water to collect in desired areas for later use, so controlling its movement and preventing soil erosion. Circular berms around the base of newly planted trees or shrubs can also help to retain water and direct it to roots. Berms can be planted to make an attractive feature and provide food and habitat for wildlife.

USING EARTHWORKS TO MANAGE WATER

CHANGING THE TOPOGRAPHY IN YOUR GARDEN ALLOWS WATER TO BE RETAINED OR SHED IN THE AREAS THAT YOU CHOOSE. WATER IS DIRECTED TO PARTS OF THE GARDEN WHERE IT IS WANTED, SUCH AS AN EPHEMERAL POND, RATHER THAN MAKING OTHER AREAS BOGGY AND IMPRACTICAL.

SWALES

These shallow, typically vegetated, channels are designed to collect and convey a shallow depth of water. They are often used in conjunction with other systems to promote infiltration of water into soil and reduce runoff. Swales can be strategically placed to guide rainwater to plants or storage systems, such as ephemeral ponds, harvesting water while creating an attractive feature.

EPHEMERAL PONDS

An ephemeral pond, like that designed for the WaterAid garden (below), is a temporary, seasonal body of water that forms after heavy rains and naturally dries up as water evaporates or infiltrates into the soil. It is an ideal addition to a rain garden, as it forms an attractive feature that can capture excess water, and provide habitat for wildlife and plants adapted to both wet and dry conditions, promoting biodiversity. When designed properly (see p.130), ephemeral ponds release water slowly into the soil, supplying moisture for plants nearby.

"AN EPHEMERAL POND PROVIDES HABITAT FOR WILDLIFE AND PLANTS ADAPTED TO BOTH WET AND DRY CONDITIONS."

[Left] Long, thin recharge trenches can gather water from large areas.
[Below] Lining a recharge trench with free-draining gravel helps water to infiltrate into the soil.

RECHARGE TRENCHES

Recharge trenches are long and linear, aimed at distributing water laterally into soil and manage larger water flows. Rainwater is directed into recharge trenches or pits either from adjacent impermeable surfaces or from a direct source, such as a disconnected downpipe. The trench or pit is filled with free-draining gravel or sand, allowing the water to percolate into the ground, which replenishes groundwater and reduces runoff.

SOAKAWAYS

In contrast to recharge trenches, soakaways are compact pits or chambers, usually filled with rubble or prefabricated units such as recycled plastic "egg crate" boxes, designed to collect rainwater and allow it to infiltrate vertically into the surrounding soil. Their main purpose is to provide drainage in a specific area, managing stormwater from roofs, driveways, or other impermeable surfaces. Commonly used in residential settings, soakaways are ideal for handling localized issues with smaller volumes of water.

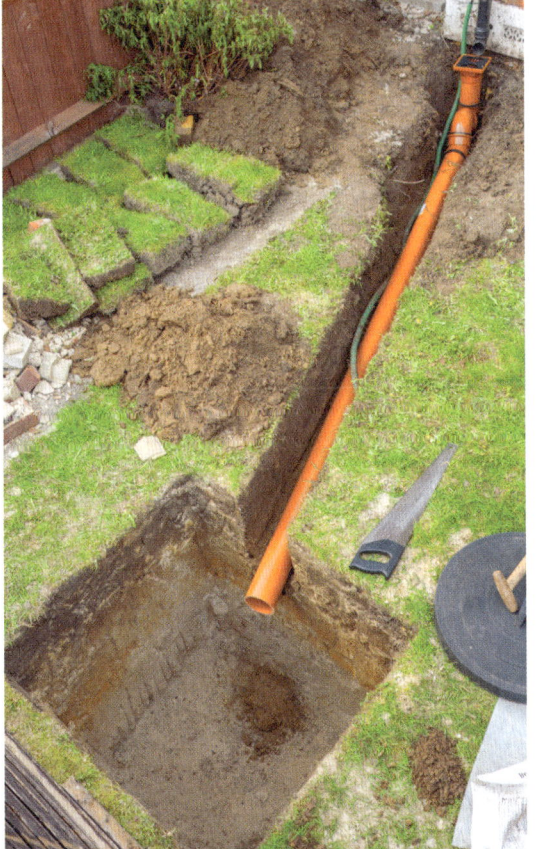

A soakaway can be useful for managing rainwater runoff from a roof, especially where space is limited.

Permeable paving can be made from many different types of materials, including clay pavers, loose gravel, resin-bound gravel, specially designed porous concrete, or interlocking concrete or stone pavers. These materials are specifically designed or specified to facilitate water infiltration.

It is also vital to lay them on a free-draining sub-base, such as sand or a granular sub-base with low levels of fine particles, because this will permit water to percolate through to the soil below.

Permeable paving is ideal for use on driveways, and especially beneficial if a front garden is being adapted to include parking, because it prevents runoff of rainwater into the street, which is a common cause of localized flooding. Taking this a step further and specifying a permeable driveway with a water harvesting tank beneath (see p.53), allows water that filters through paving to be collected and stored for garden or household use.

Interlocking precast permeable paving units provide soil-filled pockets for plants that also allow water to infiltrate.

PERMEABLE PAVING

THIS TERM REFERS TO HARD LANDSCAPED AREAS SPECIALLY DESIGNED TO ALLOW RAINWATER TO FILTER THROUGH INTO THE SOIL, OR TO BE COLLECTED IN UNDERGROUND TANKS (SEE P.50). PERMEABLE PAVING IS VITAL TO COMBAT DRAINAGE PROBLEMS AND FLOODING THAT OFTEN OCCUR AFTER HEAVY RAIN.

GREEN, BLUE, AND BIOSOLAR ROOFS

FOR DECADES, ROOFS HAVE BEEN DESIGNED OR MODIFIED TO STORE AND SLOW THE FLOW OF RAINWATER, SOMETIMES USING STORAGE TANKS AND SOMETIMES BY BLANKETING THEIR SURFACE WITH PLANTING. DESIGNERS ARE NOW EXPLORING NEW WAYS TO COMBINE THESE AND OTHER TECHNOLOGIES TO HELP MAKE OUR BUILT ENVIRONMENT MORE WATERWISE.

Green roofs, clothed with a layer of vegetation, are now a familiar concept. This can be "intensive" with larger plants and a deeper soil layer, or "extensive" with less soil and low-growing, hardier plants, like sedums. These passive harvesting systems help to manage the flow of rainwater from a roof by absorbing up to 65 per cent of rainfall and delaying the flow rate of what drains from the roof by about three hours. All this reduces pressure on drainage and sewer systems during heavy rainfall.

A blue roof has similar benefits, but is fitted with a rainwater management system that captures and temporarily stores rainwater in what are called "attenuation tanks" on the roof's surface, which then control the water's release.

Blue-green roofs are innovative systems that integrate passive green roof technology with active water management features to effectively capture, retain, and use rainwater. They combine a planted layer with layers designed for stormwater storage and management, such as attenuation tanks.

These combined technologies can be further supplemented with a "yellow" layer, where solar panels are added for energy production. Such "biosolar" roof systems employ planting to help cool the panels, which not only increases the efficiency of energy production, but also creates aesthetically pleasing areas that support urban biodiversity.

Planting on this biosolar roof reduces the temperature around its solar panels on hot days, which increases their energy output.

CHAPTER FOUR

NURTURING SOIL

SOIL AS A WATER STORE

SOIL SERVES AS A NATURAL STORE FOR THE MOISTURE ESSENTIAL FOR PLANT GROWTH AND REGULATES THE MOVEMENT OF WATER WITHIN ECOSYSTEMS. ITS ABILITY TO HOLD WATER DEPENDS ON KEY CHARACTERISTICS, SO ASSESS YOUR OWN GARDEN SOIL TO SEE HOW ITS PROPERTIES WILL IMPACT ANY WATERWISE PROJECTS OR PLANT CHOICES (SEE P.132).

SOIL TYPE INFLUENCES WATER MOVEMENT

The capacity of soil to retain water is influenced by the size of the gaps, known as "pores", between soil particles. A network of larger pores within soil provides space for water to infiltrate and drain away, while smaller pores hold on to water molecules via capillary action, meaning that water takes longer to infiltrate and is more readily retained. A balance of both these qualities is usually considered ideal for garden soil, so that it does not remain waterlogged after heavy rain, but retains enough water to supply the needs of plants.

Different soil types are characterized by their different particle sizes and the effect this has on their ability to hold water.

SOIL ORGANIC MATTER

Organic matter helps to bind soil's mineral particles into aggregates of different sizes, creating different sized pores. This enhances the soil's ability to store and drain water. Additions of organic matter benefit all soil types (see pp.94-103).

Clay soils have fine particles and many small pores that allow them to hold water well, but drainage is slow, risking waterlogging.

Loamy soils contain a mix of particle and pore sizes, so offer both good drainage and excellent water retention. This makes them ideal for most plants.

Sandy soils are made up of larger particles that create large pores, enabling water to drain away quickly, so that the soil dries out fast.

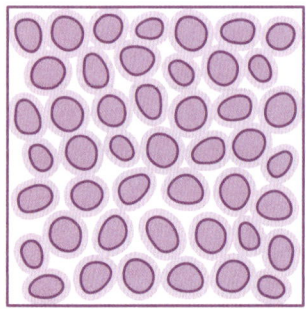 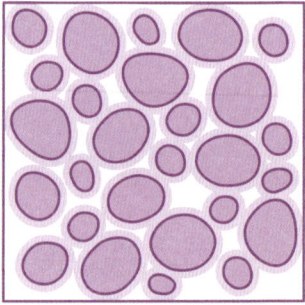 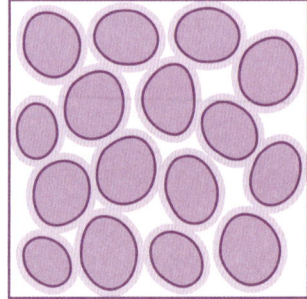

○ Water held by soil particles
○ Soil particles

AVAILABLE WATER FOR PLANTS

Not all water that falls on soil will be available to plant roots. After rainfall or irrigation, gravity moves water down to fill pore spaces within the soil. When all pores are full, soil reaches "saturation point". Once rain or irrigation stops, excess water drains to leave the soil at "field capacity", which is the maximum moisture that its pores can retain. At moisture levels below this water is available to roots, and once taken up by plants it is lost from soil via evapotranspiration. If no further water is received, soil will reach "permanent wilting point" when it has dried out to the extent that plant roots can no longer extract water. The difference between a soil's field capacity and permanent wilting point is the available water that plants can access.

WATERLOGGING

Waterlogging occurs when the soil becomes saturated with water (saturation point), leading to limited air space and the development of anaerobic conditions. The lack of air in the soil can suffocate plant roots, which need oxygen, making it difficult for them to survive.

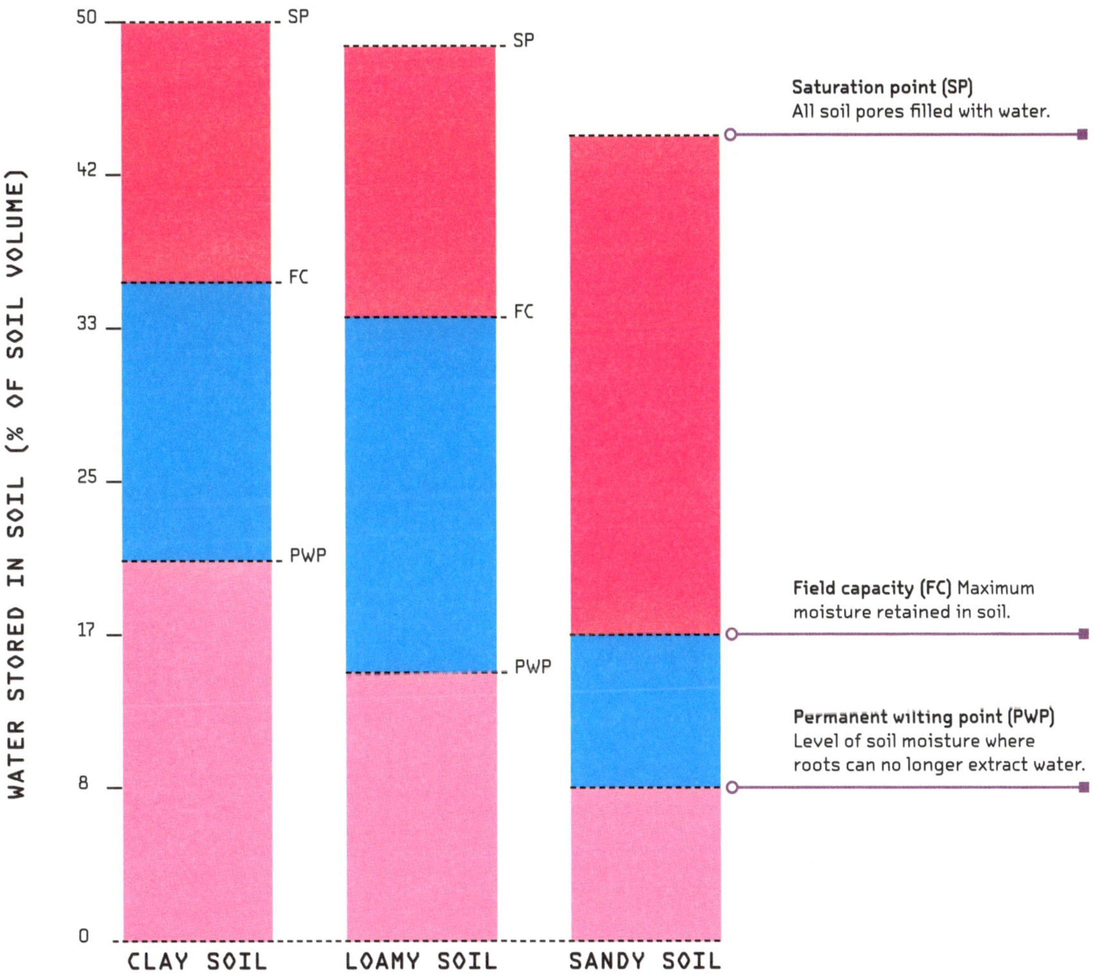

Saturation point (SP) All soil pores filled with water.

Field capacity (FC) Maximum moisture retained in soil.

Permanent wilting point (PWP) Level of soil moisture where roots can no longer extract water.

Water available to plants in three soil types
The different properties of each soil type have a huge influence on water availability to plants. Sandy soils tend to drain more quickly, limiting what is available to roots. The smaller pores of clay and loamy soils hold water, so more moisture is present to support plant growth.

- Excess water drains away
- Water available to plant roots
- Unavailable water held in soil pores

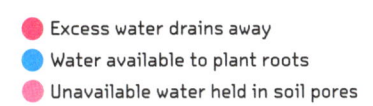

MULCHING TO BENEFIT SOIL AND PLANTS

A mulch is a layer of material applied to the soil surface. Mulching is a valuable technique because organic mulches can improve soil health, help soil retain moisture, protect soil from erosion, support beneficial organisms, and help protect soil and plants from extreme temperatures.

- **Moisture conservation** Mulches cover the soil surface, and reduce evaporation in warm, windy weather. They can also help to prevent runoff during heavy rain, allowing water to infiltrate into the soil. Coarse organic mulches conserve moisture more effectively than finer materials, which can wick water away from the soil below. Mulches also suppress weed growth, reducing competition for water and nutrients.
- **Prevention of erosion** A mulch protects soil from damage during heavy rainfall, and helps to prevent its surface drying out and being blown away. Mulches generally have a rough, open texture that allows water to trickle down and infiltrate soil, helping to stop runoff (see box) washing soil away. However, replacing ground cover plants with inorganic mulches, like gravel, can increase the risks of erosion, compaction, and waterlogging by depleting soil's biological activity.
- **Temperature regulation** A layer of mulch can insulate soil against temperature extremes and reduce plant stress caused by these fluctuations. Organic mulches, like shredded wood, excel in regulating soil temperature, while inorganic mulches, such as gravel or rubber, often increase soil and air temperatures around plants.
- **Soil health** Organic mulches improve soil health by feeding soil life, such as microorganisms and invertebrates, as they break down. This biological activity, associated with increased soil biodiversity, fosters soil health, which also benefits plant health. Over time, organic mulches will increase the carbon content of depleted soils, which enhances water infiltration and aeration (see p.101). Inorganic mulches, such as gravel or sand, do not typically contribute to soil fertility, but this can be desirable when growing plants adapted to drier, low-nutrient conditions.

WEED SUPPRESSANT MEMBRANES

While a mulch placed on a weed suppressant membrane can initially conserve soil moisture, over time soils beneath the membrane tend to become abnormally dry, damaging soil health and stressing plants. Membranes are usually made from non-biodegradable plastic, which can also pollute soil as it breaks down. If weeds are a problem, cover soil with biodegradable materials, such as cardboard, and/or a deeper layer of mulch.

03

INVEST IN YOUR SOIL BY MULCHING

SOIL IS VITAL FOR GLOBAL SUSTAINABILITY, BECAUSE IT IMPACTS FOOD SECURITY, CLIMATE REGULATION, AND BIODIVERSITY. EVERY GARDENER CAN MAKE A VALUABLE CONTRIBUTION TO SUSTAINBLY IMPROVING SOIL HEALTH BY INVESTING IN THEIR OWN COMPOSTING SET-UP AND MULCHING WITH HOMEMADE COMPOST.

RUNOFF

Runoff is the flow of water over land, after rainfall or snow melt, which not only occurs over impermeable paved surfaces, but also when soil is saturated or its surface has baked hard. Runoff can wash away soil, causing erosion, contribute to flooding, and transport pollutants into water bodies. Preventing runoff by covering soil with organic mulches or planting is key to a waterwise garden.

[01] As well as protecting soil, a layer of straw mulch can also help to insulate tender plants, such as dahlias, during winter.
[02] Weeds are suppressed in a new no dig bed by laying cardboard on soil, followed by a generous covering of homemade compost.
[03] An inorganic mulch of crushed brick, ceramic, and concrete suited the plants in the author's garden design for the Royal Entomological Society. Such recycled, mineral-based mulches can be sustainable options in the right context (see pp.96–97).

SELECTING THE RIGHT MULCH

BEFORE MULCHING YOUR GARDEN, IT'S IMPORTANT TO KNOW THE CHARACTERISTICS OF DIFFERENT MULCHES AND TO UNDERSTAND THE NEEDS OF YOUR SOIL AND PLANTS. REMEMBER YOU CAN MULCH DIFFERENT AREAS WITH DIFFERENT MATERIALS.

ORGANIC VS INORGANIC OPTIONS

Organic mulches, such as homemade compost or composted wood chippings or bark, do not need to be dug into soil because soil organisms pull them down into the soil where they feed on them. This breaks the organic materials down, enriching soil with nutrients, improving its structure, helping to retain moisture, and regulating soil temperature. These mulches need regular replenishment, usually once a year, but the benefits to the soil's water infiltration and storage capacity, along with plant health, repay this investment (see p.101). Using locally sourced organic material helps to ensure sustainability: compost made from your own garden waste (see p.102) is ideal, or "chop and drop" stems from herbaceous plants and grasses onto the soil as you cut them back, where they will break down.

Inorganic mulches, like stone, aggregates, or sand, are long-lasting and often attractive, but do not add organic matter to improve the soil. This can be beneficial when growing plants adapted to stony, nutrient-poor soils, or encouraging shorter, robust growth to help plants cope with exposed locations, such as a roof garden. Mineral mulches, such as gravel, heat up in the sun and radiate that heat back out, so should only be used among plants that can tolerate these increased temperatures.

Inorganic mulch often suits plants adapted to grow in stony, nutrient-poor soils, such as this *Citrus lumia* and drought-tolerant planting in the Lemon Tree Trust garden.

To determine the best mulch to use, consider the character of your garden or landscape and the type of plants it includes. Create a sustainable scheme by grouping plants from similar habitats together, so that they will thrive in the same growing conditions (see pp.134–135). A dry Mediterranean garden, for example, filled with drought-tolerant plants adapted to nutrient-poor soil would suit an inorganic mulch. Whereas in a moist, shady woodland garden, an organic mulch, such as leaf mould, would mimic the natural leaf litter that decomposes on a woodland floor.

MULCH APPLICATION
To maximize the benefits of a mulch, apply a 5–10cm (2–4in) layer over moist, weed-free soil. A thinner layer of compost mulch (about 2.5cm/1in) is recommended for annual no dig applications (see pp.102–103). Leave space around plant stems, as contact with mulch can cause issues with fungal disease. Thicker layers (up to 30cm/1ft deep) of inorganic mulches, such as sand, are sometimes specified if perennial weeds or soil fertility need to be more drastically regulated (see pp.104–105).

ENVIRONMENTAL CONSIDERATIONS
Some mulches can have undesirable environmental impacts if used in the wrong context. Rubble, crushed concrete, and sand are currently used to mulch high profile gardens, but these materials are not always appropriate. Drastically changing conditions, for example, by removing a healthy topsoil to create a more hostile, inorganic environment, is not a sustainable approach. When used as a mulch, crushed concrete, limestone with lots of fines (small particles), or crushed brick containing mortar, can increase soil pH, producing alkaline conditions unsuitable for many plants. Transport of these heavy materials also has a carbon footprint that should be considered.

This asparagus bed is mulched with sheep's wool as protection for soil, a slow release food source, a weed suppressant, and a deterrent for slugs and snails.

NURTURING SOIL

PLANET-FRIENDLY GARDENING

SHEILA DAS, formerly a Garden Manager at RHS Garden Wisley and now Head of Gardens and Parks at the National Trust, advocates sustainable horticulture and helped establish the RHS Planet-Friendly Gardening Campaign.

Sheila Das discusses composting and soil health with no dig gardening expert Charles Dowding at his garden. She and Charles firmly believe that healthy soil is a vital part of a sustainable and waterwise garden.

"

IS SOIL IMPORTANT IN A WATERWISE GARDEN?

Yes! Soil plays a fundamental role in the healthy cycle of water movement on Earth. Good soil structure helps to retain water in soil for long periods, making it accessible for plant growth. That very same structure also regulates water movement to slow its flow and to mitigate flooding. In short, soils help to store and transfer water where it is needed, both to enable growth and prevent damage to the environment.

HOW CAN WE HELP SOIL TO RETAIN MOISTURE?

Simply by growing plants. Plant roots play a key role in creating good soil structure, not only through their physical presence, but also because they help to feed the billions of organisms that live in soil. This can help to support mycorrhizal fungi, which develop a network of root-like fungal hyphae that transports nutrients and water around the soil ecosystem. The presence of soil microorganisms will depend upon the types of plants being grown – a diverse mix of species is often best to create a diverse subterranean community. Think of the mix of shrubs, trees, and herbaceous species at a woodland's edge, which is exactly what many gardens are comprised of!

HOW IS IT BEST TO ADD ORGANIC MATTER: DIG OR NO DIG?

The organisms in soil will incorporate organic matter laid as a surface mulch by consuming it, passing it on in forms that make nutrients available for plants and other life forms. When these organisms die, they themselves become more organic matter to feed the soil community around them, so there is no need for us to dig in organic matter. Routine digging can damage the soil so it is best avoided. Occasional soil disturbance is healthy though – imagine an animal making a hole or a human planting a tree.

IS IT BETTER TO USE ORGANIC OR INORGANIC MULCHES?

For many years we have assumed that covering the soil with a layer of mulch is the best way to conserve moisture, but it is becoming increasingly evident that covering the ground with living mulches of plants is extremely effective as the roots create complexity in the soil environment. Where it is desirable to improve soil moisture content, adding organic mulches, such as compost, helps to create the complex soil structure needed for water retention and flow as they are drawn into soil and consumed by the organisms that live there. Inorganic mulches do not benefit soil structure in this way but may suit certain situations where planting contains, for example, more drought-tolerant species or plants that will not thrive in wetter soil over winter. The choice depends on what the desired outcome is, so it is about selecting the appropriate mulch for each situation.

Root associations with mycorrhizal fungi Healthy soils are more likely to host species of mycorrhizal fungi, which connect with plant roots and deliver water and nutrients in exchange for energy-rich sugars.

"SOIL IS NOW CONSIDERED A BIODIVERSITY HOTSPOT, HOSTING AROUND 90 PER CENT OF ALL FUNGAL SPECIES AND HALF OF THE WORLD'S BACTERIAL SPECIES."

DR MARC REDMILE-GORDON

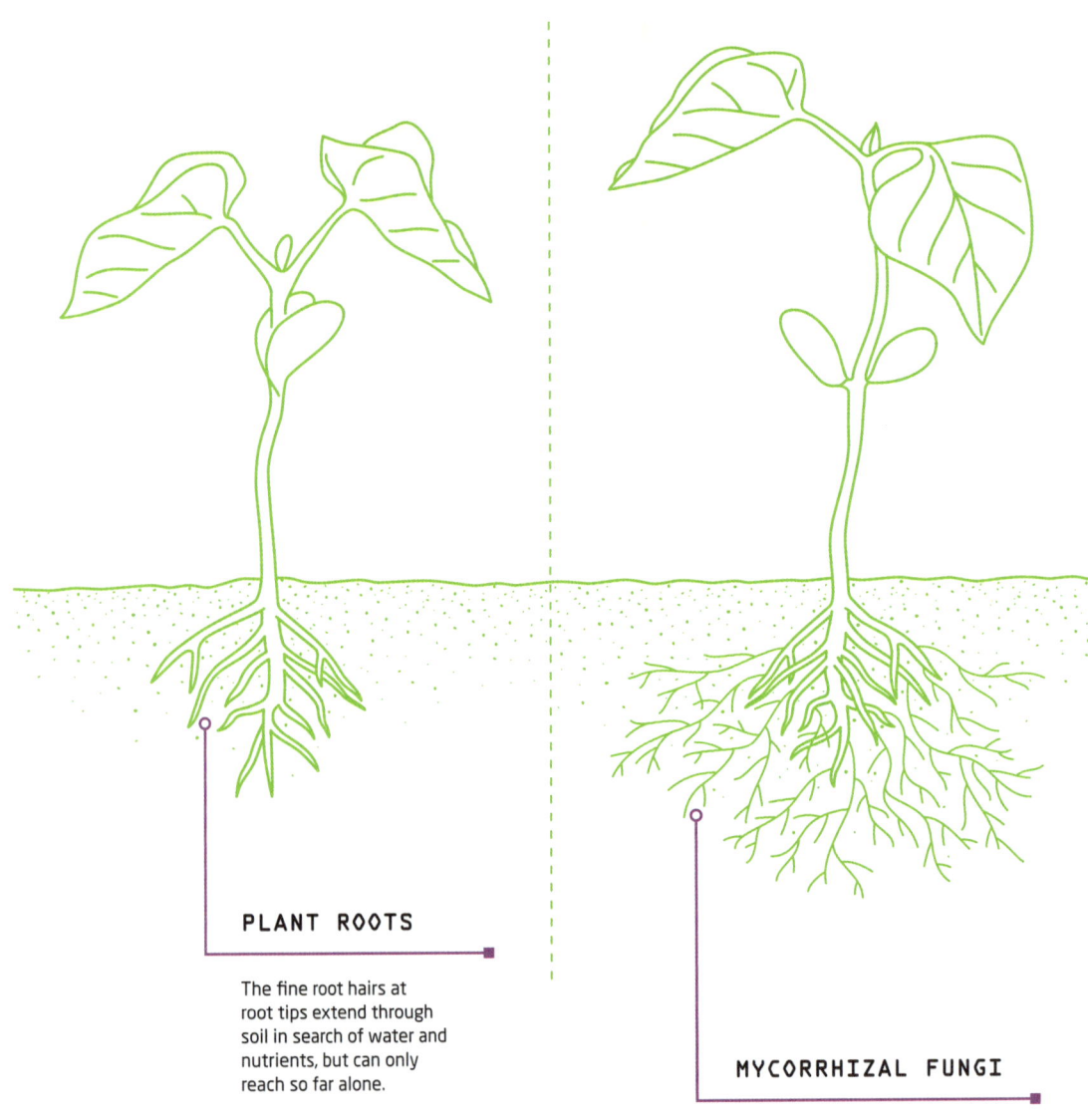

PLANT ROOTS

The fine root hairs at root tips extend through soil in search of water and nutrients, but can only reach so far alone.

MYCORRHIZAL FUNGI

Fungal hyphae that link to plant roots are finer and faster growing, allowing them to spread further and access resources that roots could not reach.

THE IMPORTANCE OF SOIL HEALTH

SOIL HAS HUGE POTENTIAL TO STORE WATER AND, IF NURTURED CORRECTLY, IT CAN ACT LIKE A SPONGE THAT CAN SIMULTANEOUSLY DRAIN AND RETAIN MOISTURE. THIS HELPS TO PREVENT DAMAGING STORMWATER RUNOFF AND SOIL EROSION, BUT CRUCIALLY ALSO ALLOWS PLANTS TO ACCESS ESSENTIAL MOISTURE, REDUCING THE NEED FOR MANUAL WATERING.

Healthy soils contain abundant organic material, which is what feeds an entire ecosystem of soil life – from microorganisms to mammals. Where ample soil organisms are eating and excreting organic matter, nutrient cycling and water retention are enhanced, both of which are crucial to supply plants with what they need for growth. Healthy soils can also act as a carbon sink, capturing the carbon in decaying plant and animal material and retaining it as soil organic matter. Nurturing soil can transform it, so it acts like a sponge that captures, retains, and drains water efficiently. This maintains a balance of water and air in soil that is vital for sustainable water management in your garden.

HOW DOES ADDING ORGANIC MATTER IMPROVE SOIL STRUCTURE?

Soil is now considered a biodiversity hotspot, hosting around 90 per cent of all fungal species and half of the world's bacterial species. Adding organic matter improves soil structure by supporting and increasing the microbial life that produces "Extracellular Polymeric Substances" – molecules that act as microbial glues. These glues bond clay particles and stabilize soil structure, keeping the pores and channels within soil open, allowing it to drain, preventing waterlogging, thereby reducing greenhouse gas emissions. Microbes also act in co-operative clusters to store water.

BENEFICIAL INTERACTIONS BETWEEN PLANTS AND SOIL LIFE

Plant roots absorb water from the soil through osmosis, via tiny root hairs at their tips. The soil microbiome – composed of bacteria, fungi, and other microorganisms – enhances water uptake not only by improving soil structure, but also by forming mutually beneficial, symbiotic relationships with plants. The best known examples of this are mycorrhizal fungi, which send networks of tiny, root-like hyphae through soil and form physical connections with plant roots so that the water and nutrients they gather can be delivered to the plant in exchange for energy-rich sugars manufactured during photosynthesis. The fungi effectively extend the plant's root network (see opposite) and increase its access to water, making it better able to cope when water is in short supply. By decomposing organic matter, soil microbes also improve the availability of nutrients to plants.

NO DIG PRACTICES NURTURE SOIL

NO DIG METHODS, USING HOME-PRODUCED COMPOST, PROVIDE A SUSTAINABLE APPROACH THAT PROTECTS SOIL STRUCTURE AND BIOLOGY, AND ENHANCES SOIL HEALTH. NO DIG IS SUITABLE WHEN GROWING FRUIT, VEGETABLES, AND MOST ORNAMENTAL PLANTS, BUT IS NOT COMPATIBLE IN AREAS WHERE AN INORGANIC MULCH HAS BEEN APPLIED (SEE PP.96–97).

MIMIC NATURAL PROCESSES

In most natural ecosystems, dead plant matter falls to the ground, where it is decomposed by soil life so that the nutrients it contains can gradually be recycled to feed other organisms. No dig gardening imitates this process by spreading a 2.5cm (1in) layer of compost on the soil surface once each year and allowing earthworms, microbes, and other soil organisms to incorporate it into the soil as they feed. This removes any need to dig or till, and prevents the disruption to soil's natural structure and its beneficial organisms that would inevitably occur. Other organic mulches, such as straw or composted wood chips, can also be used as no dig mulches.

In nature, soil is rarely left bare for long because seeds germinate and plants quickly colonize empty ground. Applying an organic mulch is enough to protect bare soil from erosion by heavy rain and strong winds, but this can also be achieved by covering the surface with plants (see box). In beds used for annual edible crops, sow green manures, such as nitrogen-fixing clover or vetch, to protect soil during winter. These will add organic matter when they are cut back and left on the soil to decompose. Permanent plant cover also protects soil and is easy to incorporate into a garden with ground cover plants or beds packed with perennials.

To start a no dig bed, a thicker 15cm (6in) mulch is often applied, in order to suppress the growth of weeds or lawn grass beneath, and to boost nutrients in depleted soil. Cardboard can be laid first as an extra barrier to weed growth.

COMPOSTING AT HOME

Composting recycles garden and kitchen waste into a valuable organic mulch that enhances soil health and plant growth. A wide range of organic materials can be composted, including lawn clippings, annual weeds, hedge trimmings, faded flowers, and plant-based kitchen scraps like vegetable peelings, as well as paper and cardboard. Combine these materials in a bin or heap, creating a balance of three parts nitrogen-rich green waste, such as grass clippings and vegetable peelings, to one part carbon-rich brown components, which include dry leaves and cardboard. Turning the pile and ensuring it is moist, but not wet, speeds up decomposition. The resulting compost is rich in microbial life and is an ideal mulch. Composting supports sustainable gardening practices and reduces landfill.

PLANTS IMPROVE SOIL PERMEABILITY

By intercepting rainfall, plants reduce the energy of raindrops and cushion the impact on the soil, minimizing compaction and erosion, while simultaneously evaporating some of the intercepted water from their leaves and stems. Through transpiration, plants draw water from the soil, creating space for additional moisture. Their root systems further enhance permeability by forming flow pathways, called macropores, which channel water deeper into the ground. Even after plants die, their decaying roots continue to benefit the soil by maintaining these pathways, further promoting water infiltration and soil health.

[Top] Pumpkins flourish in the warm, nutrient-rich, and moist conditions of a compost heap. [Above] *Phacelia tanacetifolia* (fiddleneck) growing as a green manure, before being hoed and left to decompose on the soil surface.

PLANTING IN PURE SAND

NURTURING SOIL

PETER KORN is a renowned Swedish gardener and landscape designer, known as "the sand man" for his innovative plantings in sand. These resilient gardens draw on his understanding of habitats and plant communities.

Korn blends horticulture with ecological landscape design at Klinta Garden AB, co-founded with Julia Andersson, where plants thrive in sand. This promotes plant resilience, minimizing watering.

"

WHAT ARE THE MAIN BENEFITS OF PLANTING IN DEEP SAND?

Imagine a scorching sandy beach where the surface is too hot to walk on. Yet, just a few centimetres beneath, the sand remains cool and moist, offering plants access to moisture, even in the harshest conditions. When grown in deep sand, plants develop extensive root networks, which enhances their resilience in a changing climate. The symbiosis between plant roots and mycorrhizal fungi helps the plants to obtain nutrients, minerals, and water. The reduced nutrient availability in sand also encourages slower, hardier, more durable growth, which extends plant longevity, allows stems to stand without support, and increases pest and disease resistance too. I have found that the properties of sand improve drainage and reduce the need for watering; it also reduces weeding, and the need to stake herbaceous plants.

WHAT TYPE OF SAND IS SUITABLE?

The type of sand used as a substrate or deep mulch is important; it should be coarse and well-draining to mimic natural habitats. Coarse sand provides excellent drainage while maintaining some moisture deeper below its surface, creating an environment that supports resilient plant growth. Using sand with minimal organic matter, encourages plants to develop extensive root systems that enable them to survive challenging conditions. Organic matter should also be removed from the surface of sand beds to prevent its buildup over time, compromising the sand's unique low-nutrient properties.

WHAT ARE THE DRAWBACKS?

Plants grown in conventional compost may struggle to establish in sand due to transplant shock. Creating sand beds can be labour intensive, and some fast-growing species may not thrive in such nutrient-poor conditions. Sand suits gardens mimicking arid or low-nutrient environments, such as alpine or steppe meadow-like settings. It is less suitable for plants needing richer, moisture-retentive soils.

WHEN SOURCING SAND, HOW CAN YOU MINIMIZE ENVIRONMENTAL IMPACT?

Sand is heavy and shipping it in comes at a carbon cost, especially if it is to be laid in deep layers over a large site, but this can be offset by the minimal resources needed after installation. Choose locally sourced sand to reduce its transportation impact. Do not take sand from sensitive ecosystems, such as beaches or riverbeds, to protect their biodiversity and ecological balance. Recycled materials, such as crushed concrete, may provide alternatives to sand or be used alongside it.

CHAPTER FIVE

THE WATERWISE GARDEN

THE WATERWISE GARDEN DESIGN

WHERE TO BEGIN? THE FOLLOWING PAGES ILLUSTRATE HOW CONCEPTS DISCUSSED IN EARLIER CHAPTERS CAN BE ADAPTED, EVEN FOR SMALL SPACES, BY ANALYZING EXISTING FRONT AND BACK GARDENS THAT ARE NOT MAXIMIZING THEIR WATERWISE POTENTIAL AND SHOWING HOW TO TRANSFORM THEM WITH A BEAUTIFUL, WATER-EFFICIENT DESIGN.

Many of us unknowingly waste or overlook free sources of water, which we allow to flow away. My design for the waterwise garden shows how it is possible to change the way water is harnessed and used in an ordinary garden, and aims to inspire all of us to make improvements that will reduce mains water use and stormwater runoff. Although such a full transformation may be feasible, ideas from the design can be implemented in any size garden.

KEY WATERWISE DESIGN PRINCIPLES
Follow these steps to help assess and plan how to make your garden more waterwise.

1. Make site observations
Analyze how water flows through your home and garden, identifying where it is well utilized and where wasted. Consider which water sources are available and aim to use rainwater and grey water in your garden through effective harvesting methods.

2. Start simple and at the top
Aim to collect water at the highest points possible, so your design can take advantage of gravity for easier infiltration and distribution. While pumps can be used, simpler gravity-fed systems minimize complications, energy inputs, and maintenance.

3. Slow and infiltrate water
Encourage water to soak into the soil rather than running off quickly. Several small interventions, such as permeable paving (see p.88) and earthworks (see pp.84–87), are often better at slowing flow and allowing infiltration than a single large system.

4. Design catchment areas
Exploit existing site conditions and when creating areas that collect water, make use of the excavated soil to create a range of growing conditions. For example, use higher, drier zones for pathways or dry plantings, and reserve lower, wetter zones for features like bog gardens and ephemeral ponds (see p.86).

5. Plan for overflow
Have a strategy and designated pathways to cope with excess water during heavy rainfall. Where possible, treat overflow from water tanks or rain gardens as a resource and direct it to areas where it can be used.

6. Minimize hardscaping
Opt for living and organic materials that absorb water and enhance soil water retention. Minimizing the use of hard, impermeable surfaces promotes water absorption, reducing runoff and flooding.

7. Build in adaptability
As climate patterns change, so will your water needs. Design your systems to be flexible, allowing for modifications or capacity increases as required.

The images of the waterwise garden are computer generated. For an immersive experience of the back garden design you can take a virtual tour using the adjacent QR code or by following the link: https://go.dk.com/waterwise-garden-uk

Sustainable, adaptable, and beautiful.
The waterwise garden is designed to collect,
divert, and infiltrate rainwater, creating
diverse plant habitats and inviting spaces.

SIDE-BY-SIDE COMPARISON

Plan views of the original and waterwise gardens show the contrast between impermeable hard landscaping and an inviting, planted design that captures rainwater and slows its flow.

ORIGINAL FRONT GARDEN

Completely paved and devoid of open soil or planting, this space prioritizes car parking at the expense of everything else. The drive's impermeable paving causes flooding and runoff into drains on the street, wasting usable water instead of putting it to good use.

THE WATERWISE FRONT GARDEN

Impermeable paving has been lifted and relaid on a permeable sub-base of coarse, free-draining aggregate, with planting and gravel between the slabs. A sunken rain garden captures and uses water that caused issues before, while a stepping stone path creates an engaging and visually appealing route to the front door, showing that passive water harvesting (see pp.72–89) can be exciting, while reducing runoff and flooding.

ORIGINAL REAR GARDEN

This bland, sterile space is dominated by hard landscaping, leaving very little opportunity for water to infiltrate into the soil. The hot, south-facing area near the house feels exposed and devoid of life or atmosphere. The artificial lawn is also prone to flooding due to runoff from paving and compacted, lifeless soil.

THE WATERWISE REAR GARDEN

A large ephemeral pond and rain garden capture water, allowing it to infiltrate into the soil, and creating an abundantly planted haven for wildlife that can be accessed by permeable walkways. Additional active water harvesting (see pp.44-71), using tanks and a water butt, allows rainwater from the roofs to be collected and reused.

THE WATERWISE GARDEN

FRONT GARDEN SITE ANALYSIS

When it comes to being waterwise, the original front garden is failing. The fully paved site is impermeable to water and prone to flooding; it lacks any kind of permeable surface or planting that could allow rainwater to infiltrate into the soil. No rainwater or stormwater is collected or utilized.

UNDER-UTILIZED ROOF

The roof of the bin store drains straight onto the drive's impermeable paving, exacerbating problems with flooding. This is one of several wasted opportunities to capture rainfall.

NO PLANTS OR SOIL

The garden has no soft landscaping features at all, which prevents water infiltrating into the soil. This also creates an unwelcoming, sterile environment, with no seasonal interest, colour, or wildlife value.

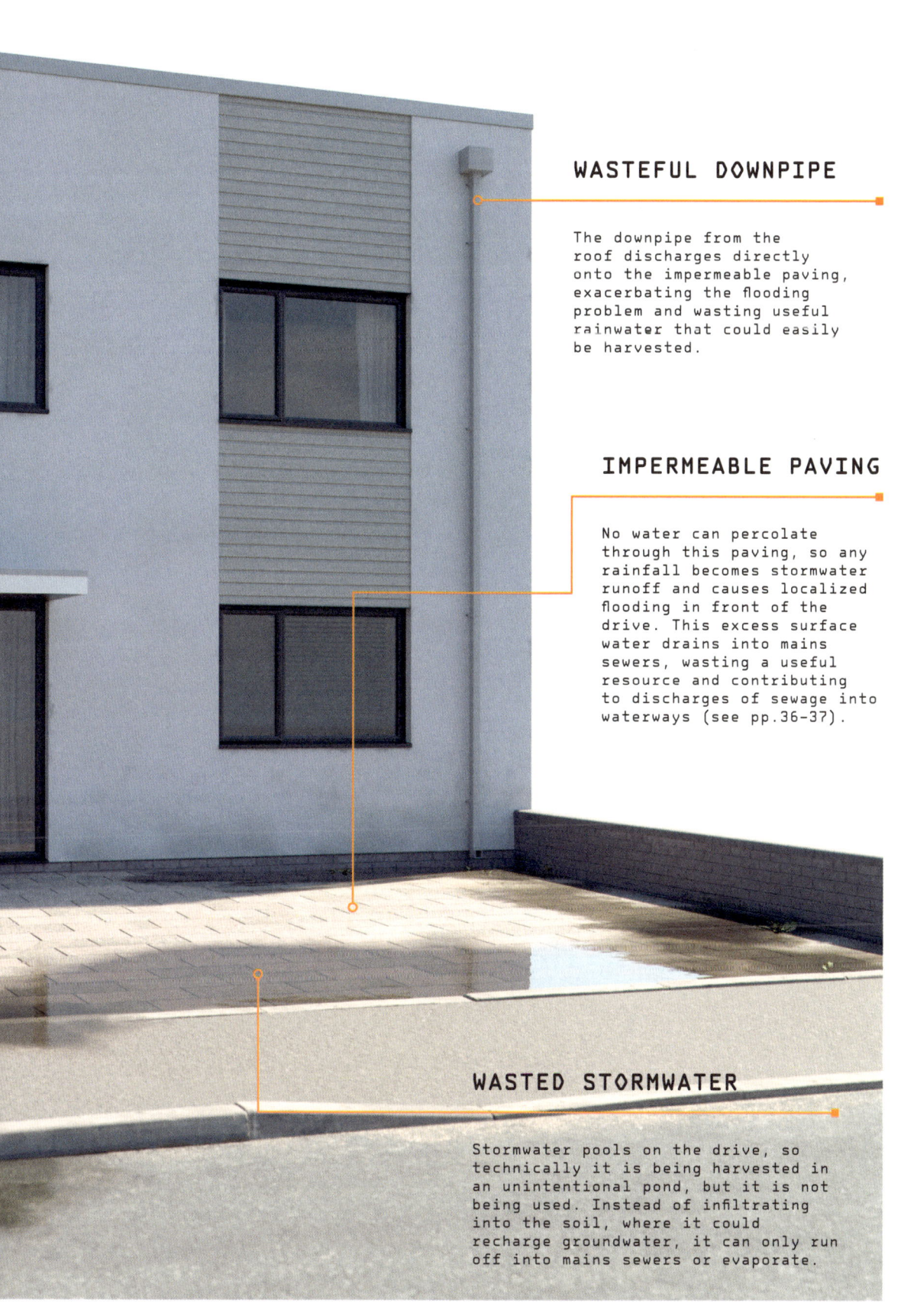

WASTEFUL DOWNPIPE

The downpipe from the roof discharges directly onto the impermeable paving, exacerbating the flooding problem and wasting useful rainwater that could easily be harvested.

IMPERMEABLE PAVING

No water can percolate through this paving, so any rainfall becomes stormwater runoff and causes localized flooding in front of the drive. This excess surface water drains into mains sewers, wasting a useful resource and contributing to discharges of sewage into waterways (see pp.36-37).

WASTED STORMWATER

Stormwater pools on the drive, so technically it is being harvested in an unintentional pond, but it is not being used. Instead of infiltrating into the soil, where it could recharge groundwater, it can only run off into mains sewers or evaporate.

FRONT GARDEN WATERWISE DESIGN

This design offers a solution that is focused on reducing flooding, while improving the water harvesting capacity of the garden. Passive rainwater harvesting methods, including a rain garden and permeable paving, are used to achieve this and create a much more attractive and biodiverse space.

GREEN ROOF

Even the smallest roof can be green. Adding a shallow layer of soil and plants slows the flow of rainwater that lands on the roof, and partially absorbs it. Any excess is directed into the rain garden via a concealed gutter and downpipe.

PASSIVE WATER HARVESTING

Replacing impermeable paving with a planted rain garden, has resolved the flooding issues, while enhancing the garden's appearance, boosting biodiversity, and providing habitat for wildlife. The rain garden (see pp.124–127) captures rainwater and stormwater from surrounding surfaces, as well as overflow from the bin store's green roof and the roof's downpipe.

TREES, PLANTS, AND SOIL

Planting dramatically improves the appearance of the garden and increases its wildlife value. It also allows rainwater to infiltrate into the soil, solving flooding issues, replenishing groundwater, and bringing life to the space. The downpipe that discharged onto impermeable paving now irrigates the garden, with the rain garden receiving overflow.

PLAYFUL LANDSCAPING

Flat-topped, locally sourced boulders, create stepping stones through the rain garden, making this functional waterwise feature more interesting and exciting by allowing closer interaction with the plants and the water.

RECYCLED PERMEABLE PAVING

Existing paving has been lifted, cut down, and relaid on a permeable base to form hard standing for a car. Water can infiltrate into planted areas and gravel. Using existing materials reduces both waste and cost.

REAR GARDEN SITE ANALYSIS

The rear garden also performs poorly from a waterwise perspective, with water badly managed and wasted across the space. Downpipes from the roof discharge rainfall into mains sewers and no harvesting systems, passive or active, are employed. The garden does include planting, but in small pots and narrow planters that dry out rapidly and need regular watering to sustain plants. Water runs off the impermeable paving and floods the lawn at its lowest point. A large side return area is underused.

ARTIFICIAL LAWN

A lifeless artificial lawn is made of plastic. Its surface can't absorb water, and does not shade or cool the soil like a living lawn. Due to poor installation, it floods at the bottom of the garden. The soil beneath is compacted and suffocated, limiting soil life and water-storing capacity.

LIFELESS VIEW

The view from the house is dull and featureless, with expansive areas of paving and lawn, and little in the way of planting or varied topography.

EXPOSED SOIL

The few plants provide limited interest and little value for wildlife. Their wide spacing in narrow raised beds leaves soil exposed so it retains little moisture and dries out quickly. Plants in raised beds and pots dry out faster than those in the ground, so need more watering, and are susceptible to pests and diseases.

EXPANSIVE PAVING

A high proportion of the garden is occupied by impermeable hard paving. This might provide practical hard standing, but it causes significant stormwater runoff, exacerbating flooding at the bottom of the garden.

WASTED WATER

Rain that falls on both of the large flat roof surfaces is channelled straight from the downpipes into mains sewers, rather than being harvested and stored for use.

UNDER-UTILIZED SIDE RETURN

A large side return area, with a downpipe carrying rainwater from the roof, offers opportunities to harvest rainwater, but is simply filled with impermeable paving.

PLANTS IN POTS

The small volume of soil in a pot heats up and dries out quickly in warm weather, which means that potted plants are water intensive, and need frequent watering. Plants in the soil need less maintenance because they can spread roots further and have better access to stored water and nutrients.

REAR GARDEN WATERWISE DESIGN

Transformed into a vibrant, waterwise oasis, the rear garden is now full of life and colour. It features a variety of active and passive rainwater harvesting systems, along with new trees and other plants chosen to thrive in the varied growing conditions that have been created.

WATER BUTT

A large water butt collects rainwater from the downpipe running from the smaller flat roof. It is fitted with an overflow that discharges any excess water into the ephemeral pond.

PERMEABLE LANDSCAPE

The lawn and impermeable paving have been replaced by permeable walkways, built from recycled steel grating and locally sourced timber, that appear to float over the garden. Water and wildlife can move freely beneath them, while planted areas capture and absorb rainwater that falls through.

EPHEMERAL POND

Rainwater is channelled into a central depression that fills with water during wet periods and dries out in warm, sunny weather. Fed solely by rainwater, this ephemeral pond (see p.130) adapts to the changing seasons, and needs no top-ups with mains water.

CREVICE GARDENS

Existing paving has been reconfigured into permeable paving and used to create crevice gardens on the sunny terrace (see p.123). Built on mounds, with paving slabs set on edge, these areas create the free-draining conditions that suit alpine plants naturally adapted to grow between rocks.

BIOSOLAR ROOF

Solar panels are fitted above green roof planting, which cools them improving their efficiency. The resulting energy can be used to run pumps in active rainwater harvesting systems.

CAPTURED RAINWATER

Rain that falls onto the large flat roof is now captured in active and passive rainwater harvesting systems. No rainfall enters mains sewers, it is all retained and utilized within the garden.

RAINWATER HARVESTING TANKS

Previously unused space now houses tanks, sized to capture rainwater from the roof. Stored rainwater is ideal for irrigation. Woven willow stems screen the plastic tanks (see p.128), and are hinged to access each tank's top.

COMPOST AREA

A hot composting bin enables the rapid transformation of green garden waste into compost (see p. 103).

HYDROPONIC GROWING SYSTEM

Simple to set up, this is a highly water- and space-efficient way to cultivate edible crops like herbs and salads (see p.129). Harvested rainwater is recirculated through the system, making it far less wasteful than watering plants in pots, where water flows out and is lost.

Permeable walkways seem to float over the garden. Water and wildlife can flow through and move beneath the recycled steel grating and timber.

THE DESIGN EXPLORED IN DETAIL
PERMEABLE WALKWAYS AND PAVING

CREATING PRACTICAL WAYS TO MOVE THROUGH A GARDEN MAXIMIZES ENJOYMENT OF THE SPACE AND CREATES ROUTES FOR MAINTENANCE AND ACCESS. HARD, IMPERMEABLE MATERIALS CAUSE RUNOFF AND DRAINAGE ISSUES, PROBLEMS THAT CAN EASILY BE AVOIDED BY CHOOSING PERMEABLE OPTIONS OR LAYING PAVING ON A PERMEABLE BASE.

PERMEABLE WALKWAYS

Thinking creatively about hard materials you could use that might have a lighter impact on the environment is important. Considering how these materials are installed and how easily they could be removed, reused, or recycled at the end of their life is important too.

In the waterwise garden open timber decking, with gaps between the boards, is raised up over the landscape, so water, wildlife, and plants can move and grow beneath. Timber is a low embodied carbon material that is renewable if from sustainable sources; check with the supplier that wood is from a certified sustainable source and locally produced if possible. Recycled timber is also an option.

Repurposed metal walkway gratings are also used in the waterwise garden, which are strong and durable as they are made from steel. Their open mesh design allows both water and light through to the soil and plants beneath.

When creating raised walkways it is important to select the right base or foundation material to create a structure that is stable. Ground screws (giant screws driven into the ground) provide solid anchor points upon which a timber, metal, or recycled plastic support framework can be constructed. Height is an important consideration when building a raised walkway, because if it is too high, safety could be compromised. Any walkway more than 60cm (2ft) from ground level should be fitted with a balustrade to protect users from falling off the edge.

DIY PERMEABLE PAVING

In my design for the waterwise garden I have suggested the fairly radical option of lifting the existing paving, cutting it down to a slimmer profile format to reduce the impermeable surface area, then re-laying it on a permeable sub-base, with permeable gravel channels between slabs.

Obviously this would be a lot of work, and it may be more realistic to improve the permeability of existing paving, rather than to lift and re-lay an entire area. This can be done by creating gaps or pockets between pavers or slabs, or by removing a few pavers and replacing them with permeable materials like gravel, sand, or soil (see p.122). The way that paving has been built up and laid will determine how easy this is to achieve.

Lifting, cutting down, and re-laying existing paving on a permeable sub-base allows much more water to infiltrate into soil.

PAVING LAID ON A SAND BED

Block paving, bricks, or pavers laid on sand should initially be permeable, but gaps between pavers can clog over time reducing permeability. It should be easy to lift out units to create planting pockets. These types of paving are usually laid on a permeable sub-base, but it is important to check by pouring water into your planting pocket to see if it drains away. This may not work on heavy clay soils or where there are other materials impeding drainage under paving, so keep the removed pavers and materials to replace if the tests fail.

- Remove a paver or pavers – focus on lifting units in areas prone to pooling.
- Dig down – create a cavity to improve drainage and remove any impermeable material.
- Add permeable material – fill the cavity with gravel, sand, or soil, which will allow water to filter through.
- Check permeability – test drainage by pouring in a bucket of water and see if it seeps away.
- If water doesn't drain – excavate further until you hit subsoil and try again.

PAVING LAID ON A MORTAR BED AND/OR A CONCRETE BASE

Most paving made up of larger slabs, for example sandstone, limestone, granite, or porcelain, will have been laid on an impermeable, compacted sub-base, or a mortar bed, sometimes with a concrete slab beneath them. These will be much harder to remove and modifications to these solid materials are likely to require machinery, such as a powered grinder or breaker. Seek assistance from an experienced landscaper if you are not confident to undertake this yourself.

It may be possible to improve the permeability of this type of paving by adding planting pockets filled with permeable materials, in the same way as paving laid on a sand bed. To do this, remove a slab carefully using a grinder or breaker, without damaging surrounding paving. Dig down to create a cavity to improve drainage and remove any impermeable material. This might involve further cutting out or breaking of concrete and the removal of a compacted granular sub-base. The cavity can then be filled with gravel, sand, or soil, which will allow water to filter through. Test drainage by pouring in water; if it doesn't seep away, excavate further and retest. Where clay soil or other materials impede drainage, this might not work.

Planted channels between paving create permeable surfaces that enhance drainage and aesthetics.

HOW TO BUILD A CREVICE GARDEN

A crevice garden is an ideal permeable addition to a sunny terrace or patio. It is created by using old paving slabs, slips of slate, or chunks of reclaimed concrete or stone to make narrow rock formations that mimic alpine environments where drought-tolerant plants thrive.

I included three crevice gardens in my design for the terrace in the rear waterwise garden, to add colour, interest, and increased permeability to this area. They are simple to construct where paving is being partly lifted, or reconfigured, to improve permeability. Once space has been created by removing slabs or blocks, start by digging a trench and positioning slabs or stones vertically, with their narrow edge facing upwards, to create a varied layout with plenty of cracks and crevices. Fill these spaces with washed sharp sand (see p.104), or a free-draining, gritty soil mix, to suit plants that don't like wet soil conditions. Select hardy, drought-resistant plant species (see p.156) and plant them directly into the crevices. Finally, mulch the surface with gravel (see p.94) to retain moisture and enhance the garden's rocky aesthetic.

Crevice gardens create topographical interest and allow alpine and succulent plants to thrive (see p.156).

MATERIALS NEEDED

- Flat stones or slabs, such as slate or sandstone
- Soil or substrate mix – washed sharp sand or a sandy, gritty soil that drains well
- Gravel or small stones for mulch
- Tough, drought-resistant plants, such as alpines or succulents
- Optional compost or topsoil for base layer

STEP 1

Prepare the area by digging a base 30–45cm (12–18in) deep to allow room for the placement of stones and plant roots.

STEP 2

Arrange the stones or slabs vertically and alongside one another to create narrow crevices. Vary stone heights and angle them slightly to mimic natural rock formations and ensure that they are stable.

STEP 3

Backfill the gaps between the stones with free-draining sharp sand or a gritty soil mix. Check that crevices are filled to ensure stability.

STEP 4

Plant drought-tolerant plants, like sedums, alpines, or succulents in the crevices. Small specimens will be easier to plant in tight gaps. Cover any exposed soil with a gravel mulch, to help retain moisture.

Rain gardens aid rainwater infiltration, and careful plant choices will boost biodiversity and support local wildlife (see p.160).

The topography of the front waterwise garden has been modified to create a rain garden (see p.82) where there was formerly an area of impermeable paving where water pooled, and which caused runoff into the street. This is simple to construct by digging a shallow depression to receive rainwater channelled from the roof of the house and the adjacent bin store, allowing it to pool and slowly infiltrate into the soil. The rain garden is lower than the nearby road, from which it can also absorb stormwater runoff, further benefitting the local environment and reducing flood risk.

Rain gardens can be simple turfed depressions, but by adding a diverse array of plants, shrubs, and trees, they can become a beautiful addition to a garden, while providing valuable habitat and shelter for wildlife. The way that landscaping interacts with the rain garden can also be playful – in the waterwise front garden, large flat-topped boulders form stepping stones that allow closer interaction with the space, and a way to move though the wet area that is particularly exciting when it is full of water!

COMMON ISSUES AND SOLUTIONS

It may sound obvious, but ensure the rain garden is lower than – or downhill from – the base of your downpipe, so that the rainwater will flow in the desired direction. Also check the levels across the slope to ensure there is no unintended overflow. Confirm that no underground utilities will be affected by excavations by carefully digging trial pits to check the site is clear. To create a rain garden on poorly draining soil, incorporate gravel or aggregates to aid drainage. Once built, test the garden's capacity to manage water flow and adjust the inflow and outflow points for water as needed, to check they can cope with heavy rainfall.

ASSESSING LOCATION AND SOIL SUITABILITY

When planning a rain garden, it's essential to locate existing underground utilities, such as gas pipes and electricity cables, so they can be avoided during excavations. If the site is less than 5m (16ft) from your home, seek professional advice from a geotechnical adviser to check that infiltrating water will not affect the building's foundations. It is also advisable to consider overflow and how this will be managed from the outset, as heavy rain could overwhelm a rain garden.

A rain garden is best located in full sun or partial shade, ideally in a well-drained area, with a gentle slope (10 per cent or less) to aid the flow of water. To determine the suitability of your soil, check its infiltration rate by digging a hole about 25cm (10in) deep and filling it with water. Monitor how long it takes the water to drain; the soil should drain at a rate of at least 1.25cm (½in) per hour for a rain garden to perform well. Sites that drain more slowly may be unsuitable, particularly those with heavy clay soils or a high water table.

THE DESIGN EXPLORED IN DETAIL
CREATING A RAIN GARDEN

CHANGING A GARDEN'S TOPOGRAPHY ENABLES WATER TO BE SHED OR RETAINED IN A CONTROLLED WAY, HELPING TO ENSURE THAT AREAS FOR WALKING, PARKING, AND RECREATION ARE WELL DRAINED. EXCAVATED AREAS CREATE FEATURES WHERE RAINWATER CAN GATHER AND INFILTRATE INTO THE SOIL, ALLOWING PLANTING AND WILDLIFE TO THRIVE.

SIZING THE RAIN GARDEN

Rain gardens are usually installed to receive rainwater from impermeable areas, such as a roof or driveway. The size of the rain garden therefore depends on the area of the impermeable surface, the soil type, and the drainage rate.

Ponding depth is the depth to which water can gather before it flows out of the rain garden and is the difference between the lowest point and the outlet or overflow – it is also the depth to which you will need to dig. Soil type (see p.92) influences the ponding depth that is suitable for a rain garden. For heavier soils with infiltration rates of less than 2.5cm (1in) per hour, a shallower rain garden with at least 8cm (3in) of ponding depth is recommended to prevent water standing for long periods. On lighter soils, which drain faster, ponding depths of 8–15cm (3–6in) work well.

A general guideline is to allocate 20 per cent of the impermeable area for the rain garden. This can also be adjusted to account for ponding depth by dividing the area of the impermeable surface by 10 for an 8cm (3in) ponding depth, or by 20 for a 15cm (6in) depth. The final rain garden size can be adjusted according to specific site conditions, but as with all rainwater harvesting systems, too much capacity is always better than too little.

CREATING THE RAIN GARDEN

Outline the desired shape using a garden hose or stakes; creating an asymmetric outline will give a more organic feel, but you can be creative with the shape depending on the style of your outside space. Remove existing vegetation and dig to create a saucer-shaped depression with a flat base. Use the excavated soil to form a mound, known as a berm (see p.84), around the three lowest sides of the depression. Compact the soil in the berm to ensure it retains the pooled water. Dig a channel through the berm to create a gravel-filled overflow that will allow any excess water to drain from the rain garden in a controlled way. Add organic matter, ideally homemade compost or leaf mould, to the soil throughout the rain garden to enhance its structure (see p.101) and help it act like a sponge to infiltrate water.

WATER MANAGEMENT

To direct water from a downpipe to the rain garden, create a channel using an impermeable material, such as reclaimed half round gutter, bricks, or stone setts. Place aggregates, cobbles, or gravel at the point where water enters the rain garden to help prevent soil erosion. Use the same approach at the overflow point to stop the berm being eroded as water flows out of the rain garden.

PLANTING YOUR RAIN GARDEN

Design the garden to be visually appealing throughout the year from all angles. Plant moisture-loving species (see p.170) near the water inlet, and those that can cope with both wet and dry soil conditions (see p.160) in the rest of the area, being careful to select those that attract pollinating insects and provide a range of seasonal interest with foliage, flowers, berries, and bark. After planting, apply a mulch to the soil (see p.96), using either an organic material or a mineral mulch, like washed gravel. Plant during spring or autumn, when cooler conditions reduce the need to water plants while they establish.

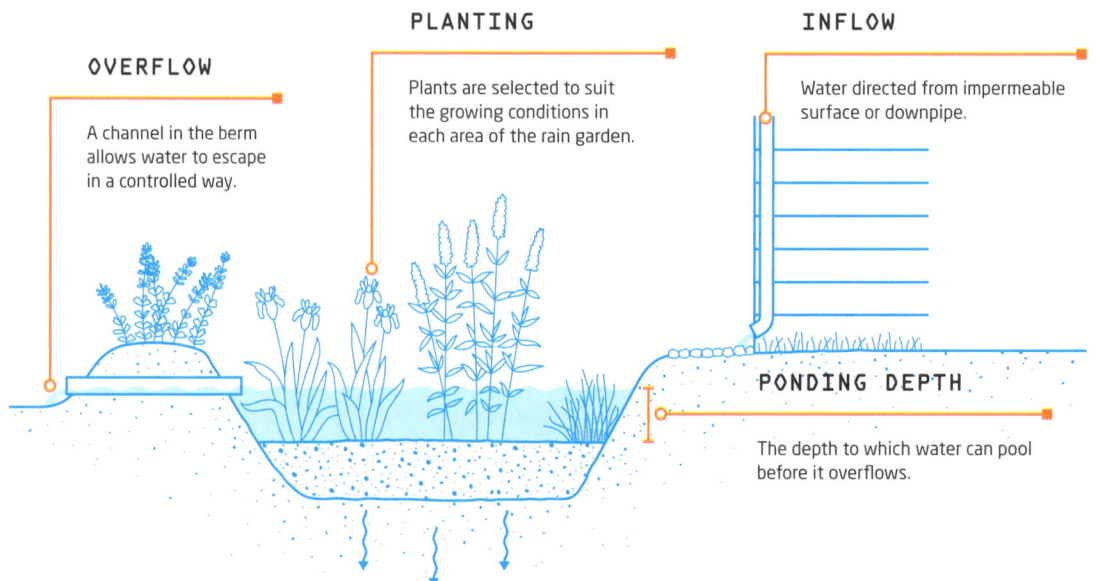

OVERFLOW
A channel in the berm allows water to escape in a controlled way.

PLANTING
Plants are selected to suit the growing conditions in each area of the rain garden.

INFLOW
Water directed from impermeable surface or downpipe.

PONDING DEPTH
The depth to which water can pool before it overflows.

[Above] Overflow from the water butt is directed into the rain garden through a pipe, ensuring no water goes to waste. [Right] Varied planting, with drought-tolerant species on dry raised berms and moisture-loving plants in wetter depressions, adds visual interest and reduces the need for watering.

THE DESIGN EXPLORED IN DETAIL
IMPROVE THE APPEARANCE OF WATER BUTTS

LARGE AND OFTEN UNATTRACTIVE, THE APPEARANCE OF WATER BUTTS AND RAINWATER HARVESTING TANKS CAN DETER GARDENERS FROM FITTING THEM, DESPITE THE BENEFITS. THERE ARE, HOWEVER, MANY WAYS TO IMPROVE THEIR LOOKS OR HIDE THEM FROM VIEW, JUST REMEMBER TO LEAVE ACCESS TO THE TAP!

Use your imagination when creating a cover or screen for rainwater harvesting tanks, because many materials are suitable. Your choice may depend on the garden style, cost, durability, and tank size. Use organic or reclaimed materials if possible to reduce waste and carbon emissions.

Reclaimed or sustainable timber will create sleek slatting or rustic cladding and can provide an attractive, long-lasting cover for any setting.

Weathering steel turns a deep rust-brown that often blends well in outdoor spaces. Reclaimed steel avoids the hefty carbon footprint of newly manufactured steel, if suitably sized sheets or items, such as old water tanks, can be found.

Climbing plants provide a beautiful screen of flowers and foliage and are best grown on a frame, rather than directly on a tank, to ensure good access and keep plant material out of stored water.

Covers can be made from organic materials, such as coppiced willow or hazel, rope, jute, hessian, twine, or wool. While natural and biodegradable, they are not durable in the long term. Reclaimed synthetic materials last longer, but can leach toxins into the soil as they break down.

In the waterwise garden, woven stems of coppiced willow (*Salix*), form a textural, sustainable screen for the rainwater harvesting tanks and water butt.

A hydroponic system can be arranged on a vertical frame, to maximize the growing potential in a small space.

A simple hydroponic system is straightforward to set up using readily available materials and equipment. Harvested rainwater can be used, further enhancing sustainability, but it is necessary to filter water and monitor pH to ensure plant health and prevent blockages. Nutrients also need to be added to the water to facilitate plant growth.

Find a location with plenty of light, but protect systems from temperature fluctuations, which can affect water quality and nutrient availability. Shield water tanks from sunlight to prevent algal growth. A pump is essential to circulate water, which needs a reliable power source – explore renewable options, such as solar power.

THE DESIGN EXPLORED IN DETAIL
HYDROPONIC GROWING SYSTEM

HYDROPONIC SYSTEMS RECIRCULATE NUTRIENT-RICH WATER DIRECTLY TO PLANT ROOTS WITHOUT SOIL, AND ARE A WATERWISE WAY TO GROW EDIBLE CROPS.

MATERIALS NEEDED

- PVC round pipe gutters and end caps
- Water pump
- A reservoir (water tank)
- Net or plastic pots
- Growing medium (expanded clay pebbles, known as Leca)
- PVC tubing and connectors
- Timber or wall brackets

STEP 1

Cut the gutters to the desired length and attach end caps. Drill evenly spaced planting holes along the top to fit the net or plastic pots. Create a timber support frame for the gutter lengths or mount brackets on a wall or fence. Fix gutters sloping slightly downwards to permit water to flow.

STEP 2

Install the water pump in the reservoir. Attach tubing from the pump to a connector in the end cap at the highest end of the gutter. Connect all gutter sections with tubing so water can flow down to the reservoir to be pumped back up.

STEP 3

Place a pot filled with soilless growing medium, such as Leca (see above), in each gutter hole. Use bare root plants or rinse soil from the roots and gently place them in pots.

STEP 4

Fill the reservoir with water and the correct dose of nutrient solution for your plants. Turn on the pump to circulate water through the system.

THE DESIGN EXPLORED IN DETAIL
BUILDING AN EPHEMERAL POND

AN EPHEMERAL POND IS A TEMPORARY, SEASONAL BODY OF WATER THAT FORMS AFTER HEAVY RAINS AND NATURALLY DRIES UP AS WATER EVAPORATES OR INFILTRATES INTO SOIL. THE EPHEMERAL POND IN THE WATERWISE GARDEN PASSIVELY HARVESTS RAINFALL FROM THE HOUSE AND GARDEN, AND RECEIVES OVERFLOW FROM THE WATER BUTT.

Designing and building an ephemeral pond creates a seasonal, sustainable, rain-fed water feature that supports wildlife and reduces garden runoff. These ponds are unsuitable for fish, as they dry up over warmer months, but mimic natural wetlands and make ideal breeding grounds for amphibians, and habitat for insects and other wildlife.

Unlike traditional water features, ephemeral ponds are designed to dry out naturally and do not need unsustainable top-ups from mains water supplies. They are also simpler to build, because a waterproof liner does not need to be fitted over the whole pond area to retain water year-round, although part of the pond can be lined so that it holds water for longer. Typically an ephemeral pond differs from the water-filled depression in a rain garden because it is deeper, larger, and generally holds water for longer, especially when built in areas where soil drains less freely.

STEP 1

Select a location away from existing trees (roots will impede excavations), ideally where rainwater naturally collects and gradually drains.

STEP 2

Dig a shallow depression with gradually sloping sides to allow easy entry and exit for wildlife. Make one side deeper (about 45–60cm/18–24in) to create varying water levels to accommodate different animal and plant life. Use excavated soil to form raised banks (berms) that will help retain water and create areas with different planting conditions.

STEP 3

To retain water in part of the pond for longer, line that area with a layer of sand, followed by a pond liner, which can be perforated to allow some infiltration. Or, where soil drains freely, use compacted clay-rich soil to form a less permeable lining.

STEP 4

Add rocks, logs, and other features at the pond's edges to create habitats and resting areas for animals. These can also conceal the edges of a liner.

STEP 5

Let the pond fill with rainwater naturally. Avoid adding tap water, as this can introduce chemicals and nutrients that will affect water quality.

STEP 6

Plant moisture-loving plants around the pond edge and in lower areas where soil remains wetter (see p.170). Choose plants well adapted to drier conditions for locations higher on the berms (see p.148).

Ephemeral ponds fill and empty with seasonal rainfall, allowing water to naturally infiltrate into the soil – a stark contrast to traditional ponds that often need top-ups from mains water supplies.

CHAPTER SIX

WATERWISE PLANTING

XERISCAPING

This waterwise landscaping technique minimizes or eliminates the need for irrigation, making it ideal for arid or drought-prone regions. By carefully selecting drought-tolerant plants that suit the local climate and using efficient watering practices, xeriscaped landscapes can thrive and be visually appealing with little or no water input, even in areas with low rainfall.

[Top] Moisture-loving *Primula beesiana* and *Osmunda regalis* are among plants chosen by Beth Chatto to suit her bog garden in Essex.
[Above] A xeriscaped scheme for a hot climate, planted with drought-tolerant aloes, *Eschscholzia californica*, and *Cleistocactus*.

RIGHT PLANT, RIGHT PLACE, RIGHT PURPOSE

SELECTING PLANTS THAT ARE NATURALLY SUITED TO THE CONDITIONS IN EACH AREA OF YOUR GARDEN WILL HELP TO ENSURE HEALTHY GROWTH AND MINIMIZE THE NEED FOR WATERING. CONSIDER SOIL TYPE, CLIMATE, SUNLIGHT EXPOSURE, SHADE, AND MOISTURE AVAILABILITY AND USE THE PLANT DIRECTORY AT THE END OF THIS CHAPTER TO FIND PLANTS ADAPTED TO THRIVE IN ALL PARTS OF YOUR GARDEN.

A waterwise garden often features diverse growing conditions, such as sunny, free-draining mounds and moist, shaded depressions. These different habitats suit different plants, so taking care to choose plants that are well adapted to the specific conditions where they are planted enables them to thrive naturally without excessive watering.

In order to achieve this, study every aspect of your site carefully. Assess the local climate, the likelihood of frosts, rainfall patterns, soil type and pH, along with any shade cast by buildings, tall trees, or hedges. Then look in more detail at how soil moisture, exposure to sun and wind, and level of shade vary in different areas, or zones, of the site. Take time to find native plant species that grow in conditions like those in your garden, along with non-native plants adapted to similar habitats around the world, as they will require little or no maintenance or watering once established, while enhancing biodiversity by providing habitat and food for wildlife. Consider the purpose of your plantings too. What are you trying to achieve – perhaps shading or cooling – and how can the plants you choose help with this?

This chapter highlights how to choose and combine plants so that you can take advantage of the same waterwise strategies that have been used in the waterwise garden design. The Plant Directory (see pp.146–181) will guide you in selecting plants that will thrive in different garden areas with little or no additional watering, creating a resilient, waterwise, and ecologically diverse landscape.

HYDROZONING

Grouping plants based on their water needs is known as "hydrozoning". This technique is essential for creating a waterwise landscape, because clustering plants with similar water requirements together in zones with suitable growing conditions means they are less likely to need watering, and effective watering is simpler and more efficient if required. This allows hydrozoning to reduce water use, enhance plant health, and reduce the need for maintenance. A good way to start is to group plants with natural associations, such as those from similar climates like Mediterranean or semi-arid, or that colonize particular habitats, such as woodlands, prairies, meadows, or rocky slopes.

NATURAL EPHEMERAL PONDS
Temporary ponds filled by seasonal rains are home to a diverse range of plant and animal species that often thrive in areas that are alternately flooded and drought prone. Many ephemeral pond plants have specific adaptations to cope with these changes, such as water-storing tissues or deep root systems, and their natural resilience can be used to design spaces that withstand fluctuating moisture levels without irrigation. Integrating native species can also help to boost local biodiversity. Ephemeral pond ecosystems can provide inspiration for rain gardens, swales, and depressions, where stormwater is captured and infiltration encouraged in a similar way.

PLANTS IN URBAN ENVIRONMENTS
Brownfield sites, canal and railway margins, and city parks often subject plants to harsh conditions, such as compacted soils, pollution, extreme temperatures, limited moisture, and physical disturbances. Any vegetation that thrives in these areas offers valuable insights for resilient waterwise planting design, because it is likely to be tolerant of heat, drought, and poor soil. Using these adaptable plants in designed landscapes can lead to robust, resilient green spaces that require fewer resources and support local biodiversity.

DRY BANKS AND ROADSIDE VERGES
These often overlooked areas typically have limited soil, low fertility, and are subject to extreme conditions like drought, compaction, and pollution. Yet despite this, tough wildflowers, grasses, and other plant species are often able to form thriving plant communities under these conditions. Their resilience in an environment with minimal nutrients and water offers valuable ideas for sustainable waterwise planting in areas with poor soil and periods of drought.

ALLUVIAL LANDSCAPES
Formed when periodic flooding of rivers deposits sediment across floodplains, alluvial landscapes have fertile soils that support diverse plant and animal life. These landscapes and their plant communities offer valuable insights for erosion control, flood mitigation, and water management, as well as inspiration for plants suited to wetter areas of rain gardens or ephemeral ponds. These natural systems demonstrate how periodic flooding can rejuvenate soil, suggesting that controlled flooding or the restoration of seasonal wetlands can improve soil health and create resilient habitats.

NATURAL GRASSLANDS AND GRAZED MEADOWS
These landscapes are home to a mix of grasses and wildflowers that thrive in nutrient-poor soils and open spaces, along with many animals, including insect pollinators and small mammals. Regular grazing maintains plant diversity by preventing the spread of shrubs and trees, and can be replicated by scything, strimming, or mowing. Plants native to grassland can be used to create ecologically rich, sustainable meadows that require minimal irrigation. Grazed meadows offer an excellent model for designing resilient, waterwise, species-rich lawns that enhance biodiversity and can better withstand drought conditions than conventional lawns.

INSPIRATION FROM NATURAL LANDSCAPES

OBSERVING WHAT GROWS LOCALLY TO YOUR SITE, OR IN LANDSCAPES WITH SIMILAR CONDITIONS TO THOSE YOU WANT TO RECREATE, IS A VALUABLE WAY TO GAIN INSIGHTS INTO THE PLANTS THAT WILL BE WELL ADAPTED TO FLOURISH IN EACH AREA OF YOUR GARDEN.

01

[01] **An ephemeral pond** in southern Spain demonstrates the diverse range of trees, shrubs, and perennials that this ever-changing natural habitat can support.

[02] **Urban landscapes** are inhabited by plants that display incredible natural resilience, such as this common chicory (*Cichorium intybus*) emerging from a crack in the pavement.

[03] **A dry cliff face** beside a railway line in Dawlish, South Devon, is clothed with the colourful garden escapee *Osteospermum* (African daisy), alongside native plants.

[04] **An alluvial river bank** in Holland is home to a willow (*Salix*), which thrives whether its roots are exposed or submerged.

[05] **A natural meadow** on Anglesey, Wales, teems with moisture-loving plant species, such as orchids and bird's foot trefoil, that could replace or enhance a traditional lawn.

WATERWISE PLANTING

SWITCHING TO NO IRRIGATION

TROY SCOTT SMITH is Head Gardener at the National Trust's Sissinghurst Castle Garden. By adopting a no-irrigation policy, he and his team are shaping the future of responsible heritage garden management.

In the Delos Garden at Sissinghurst, designed by Dan Pearson, the use of limestone aggregates has improved the drainage of the heavy clay soil, helping drought-tolerant plants to survive the wet winters.

"

WHY DID YOU STOP WATERING? IT CAN'T HAVE BEEN AN EASY DECISION, ESPECIALLY IN THE RECORD-BREAKING UK HEATWAVE OF 2022.

When I thought about the future, I found it hard to reconcile maintaining a garden that relied on significant inputs of water to look good. When viewed through the prism of climate change it was clear to me that we needed to adapt not only how we garden, but also how our garden may look in the future, to minimize the need for additional watering.

Sissinghurst is a Grade I listed garden that is considered part of our country's living cultural heritage and, given this status, I could make the case for the installation of irrigation infrastructure to protect and sustain the heritage planting schemes. On balance, however, I feel we have an opportunity to lead from the front in shaping how our heritage gardens, in particular 20th-century flower gardens, evolve so that they remain relevant and compelling as destinations and works of art. It is not just the plants, but their arrangement and management that provides the unique character and distinctive qualities of Sissinghurst's garden. This allows us to think of resilient derivatives and alternatives that retain the emotional intensity of Vita Sackville-West and Harold Nicolson's original garden.

HOW IS THIS CHANGING YOUR MANAGEMENT OF THE GARDEN?

We are looking at how best to harvest rainwater, then store and deliver it to the garden efficiently and sustainably. More trees are being planted within the garden; although they will take up water, a tree canopy will provide a gentler environment for plants than an open, sunny aspect. The collection of old roses (bred pre-1867) is being adapted to include more subtropical and China roses. Drainage is also being installed along all our historic yew hedges.

We now sow hardy annuals in autumn, rather than late February, so they can be planted out in early February when the ground is reliably moist. Tender perennials and biennials that need extra irrigation are now often replaced by more resilient perennials. Plants now need to cope with drought and increased winter wet.

HOW HAS THE DELOS GARDEN, INSPIRED BY A GREEK ISLAND, PERFORMED SINCE ITS 2019 REINSTATEMENT?

The most fundamental intervention was sharp drainage laid above, and terraced over, our heavy clay soil. Planted in this are Mediterranean species adapted to reduce water loss in their hostile native landscapes. During drought, they remain healthy and go on flowering when other plants are showing signs of stress. But these plants would suffer in Sissinghurst's wet winter soil without sharp drainage at their roots. This ensures the presence of oxygen that their extensive root systems and specialist mycorrhizal fungi rely on. Each winter more of the species we watch nervously appear increasingly robust – evidence that symbiotic relationships have flourished to give resilience to the extremes of both summer and winter.

WATERWISE PLANT ADAPTATIONS

PLANTS HAVE EVOLVED MANY INGENIOUS ADAPTATIONS TO ALLOW THEM TO SURVIVE EXTREME CONDITIONS. LEARNING TO RECOGNIZE SOME OF THESE ADAPTATIONS CAN HELP TO SELECT PLANTS THAT WILL GROW WELL IN PARTICULAR CONDITIONS AND IS A GOOD WAY TO BUILD A DEEPER UNDERSTANDING OF WATERWISE PLANTING DESIGN.

POST-PLANTING CARE

Watering is important after planting because it helps to settle soil around roots and ensures plants have moisture while their roots grow and establish. A single, thorough watering is better for plants than repeatedly watering lightly. It also reduces water use. When moisture penetrates deeply into the soil it encourages the growth of strong, deep roots. Wetting the soil surface promotes shallow rooting, making plants more susceptible to drought and less resilient in the long term.

ROOT SYSTEMS AND WATER ACCESS

Plants can only access a proportion of the water in soil (see p.93), so they have evolved complex root systems to make maximum use of this precious resource. In order to find sufficient water to supply their needs many plants have evolved deep roots and broad root systems that spread over a wide area, making them more drought tolerant. Plants will also develop according to their immediate growing conditions, and where water is abundant at the soil surface may only develop shallow roots (see box). For roots in waterlogged or flooded areas, the lack of air in soil means that accessing oxygen becomes more of a priority than water.

Two types of root systems are commonly found in plants; fibrous root systems and taproot systems (see opposite). Each of these has characteristics that help roots access water from different layers within the soil. Some plants are also able to develop adventitious roots (see opposite), which provide resilience to difficult or changing conditions. Selecting plants that are adapted to suit each area of your garden reduces the need for watering.

FIBROUS ROOT SYSTEMS

Fine fibrous roots spread widely from a plant's base through the surface layers of soil, forming a dense, mat-like root system that is highly effective at absorbing surface water and preventing soil erosion, but less able to access deep water during droughts.
Examples Grasses, ferns, palms, corn (*Zea mays*)

Rough meadowgrass (*Poa trivialis*)

TAPROOT SYSTEMS

A taproot is a single, thick, deep-growing root with smaller lateral roots extending out from it. Taproot systems enable plants to utilize deep groundwater, increasing drought tolerance, and provide excellent anchorage for plants in windy locations. Plants also use fleshy taproots to store food reserves.
Examples Wild carrot (*Daucus carota*), mullein (*Verbascum bombyciferum*)

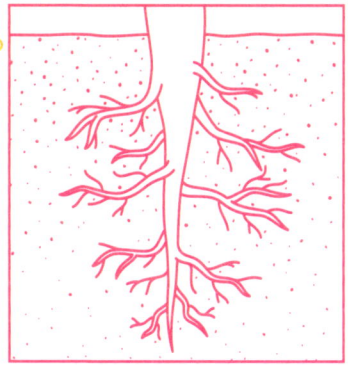

Wild carrot (*Daucus carota*)

ADVENTITIOUS ROOTS

These unbranched roots emerge rapidly from stems, leaves, or even bark, often as a response to stress or environmental conditions. Strawberries form them on long stems known as runners or stolons. They help plants access surface water, replace existing roots unable to function in flooded soil, or help stabilize plants in challenging environments.
Examples Willow (*Salix*), strawberry (*Fragaria*), periwinkle (*Vinca*)

Adventitious roots

Alpine strawberry (*Fragaria vesca*)

ADAPTATIONS TO DROUGHT OR EXTREME HEAT

These visible adaptations illustrate the remarkable resilience of plants to challenging environments with low rainfall, shallow soils, or extreme heat, such as this crevice garden. Plants have developed a range of evolutionary strategies for accessing or conserving every drop of available water; some have just one, while others combine several.

SHEDDING LEAVES
Some plants drop their leaves or become dormant when water is scarce and regrow when water becomes available.

WAX-COATED LEAVES
Some drought-tolerant plants have a thick waxy layer (cuticle) covering their leaves, which acts like a seal to reduce water loss.

HAIRY LEAVES
Tiny hairs trap a layer of humid air close to a leaf's surface, reducing the rate at which water vapour is lost through leaf pores via transpiration.

DEEP ROOTS
Many drought-resistant plants develop extensive root systems or have long taproots to access water held deep in the soil.

AROMATIC FOLIAGE
Essential oils create a protective barrier that helps to minimize evaporation rates from leaves. They also deter herbivores and pests, preventing damage and associated water loss.

REDUCED LEAF SIZE
Minimizing leaf surface area, by evolving small or needle-like foliage, reduces the leaf area exposed to drying wind and intense sunlight and so keeps water lost via transpiration to a minimum.

SUCCULENT LEAVES AND STEMS
Some plants, many known as succulents, have the ability to store water in thickened leaves or stems, allowing them to survive prolonged dry spells.

REFLECTIVE LEAF COLOUR
Plants from hot, dry habitats often have grey or silvery leaves, which reflect some of the sun's heat and reduce water loss.

ADAPTATIONS TO WET CONDITIONS AND FLOODING

The characteristics of plants that have evolved to thrive in areas of heavy rainfall and waterlogged soil are not always as easy to see as those from dry regions, but there are still numerous useful signs to look for when sourcing plants for wet areas of the garden, like this ephemeral pond. Other invisible adaptations are fascinating to discover.

LONG, FLEXIBLE STEMS
Taller plants can hold their leaves above the water level and flexible stems can flex in water currents without being damaged.

FLOOD TOLERANCE MECHANISMS
Certain species can tolerate temporary flooding by slowing down growth or altering their metabolism.

DENSE, SHALLOW ROOT SYSTEMS
Mat-like roots help to secure the plant and prevent soil washing away. Keeping roots near the surface means they will regain access to oxygen faster as soil dries out.

ADVENTITIOUS ROOTS
Plants can produce these roots rapidly, from stems or leaves above the soil or water level, allowing them to access oxygen when the existing root system is submerged.

AERENCHYMA
Some plants develop air-filled spaces in their above-ground tissues to supply oxygen to roots that would otherwise suffocate in saturated soils. These can also allow the leaves of submerged plants to float.

GLOSSY, LEATHERY LEAVES
Tough, shiny foliage repels moisture, preventing its weight damaging leaves and bacteria and fungi multiplying to cause disease. Leaves are often large to maximize photosynthesis.

SWOLLEN ROOTS AND UNDERGROUND STORAGE ORGANS
Nutrients are often limited in wet soils, so at the end of the growing season plants relocate nutrients and carbohydrates to store below ground, ready to fuel spring growth.

Certain low-growing, drought-tolerant plants, like creeping thyme (*Thymus* spp.), can create resilient, fragrant, and colourful alternatives to grass lawns.

PLANTING WATERWISE LAWNS

WITH NO FORMAL LAWN, THE WATERWISE GARDEN HAS AMPLE SPACE FOR PASSIVE RAINWATER HARVESTING FEATURES AND PLANTING. ITS ELEVATED WALKWAYS AND PERMEABLE PAVING PROVIDE WELCOMING SPACES TO MOVE AND RELAX. BUT WHERE A LAWN IS DESIRED, THERE ARE ALTERNATIVES TO TRADITIONAL LAWN GRASSES THAT CAN CREATE A MORE WATERWISE CARPET OF GREEN.

Lawns are part of the traditional garden aesthetic in many countries, and are also popular because they provide a comfortable, open space to sit or play. But maintaining a perfect green sward requires a lot of work, and lawns will turn brown in summer due to drought, heat, improper watering, and poor soil conditions. Cool-season grasses (see right) are naturally adapted to turn brown when moisture is in short supply during hot, dry spells, and green up again when rain falls. To counteract this and remain green throughout summer, many lawns will need a lot of care and attention, including regular, thorough watering during a season when there may be severe pressures on water supplies. It is also important to maintain healthy soil that is regularly aerated, to reduce compaction and aid drainage, which can help to avoid damaging root rots.

To reduce maintenance and water use, looking beyond monocultures of grass species can make lawns more resilient, biodiverse, and drought tolerant. Many plant species also stay green in dry conditions, reducing the need for watering to maintain that aesthetic. It is possible to use certain plants, such as creeping thyme (*Thymus serpyllum*), as a lawn substitute, because they are able to tolerate light foot traffic. Other drought-tolerant plants, such as white clover (*Trifolium repens*), bird's foot trefoil (*Lotus corniculatus*), or yarrow (*Achillea millefolium*), can be added to grass lawns both to stay green in dry conditions and to increase their diversity and wildlife value (see pp.178–181).

Allowing lawns to grow taller improves their resilience to drought, because the longer shoots will be balanced by deeper roots, which can access water from deeper in the soil. Taller plants also shade the soil, reducing surface evaporation.

CHOOSING THE RIGHT LAWN GRASS

In temperate regions, lawns are traditionally made up of cool-season grass species, which typically thrive between 15°C (59°F) and 24°C (75°F). They grow best in spring and autumn when conditions are moist and milder, and will become dormant and brown during prolonged hot, dry periods, especially when water is limited. These grasses include Kentucky bluegrass (*Poa pratensis*), perennial ryegrass (*Lolium perenne*), and various fescues (*Festuca* spp.).

In contrast, warm-season grasses, such as zoysia grass (*Zoysia* spp.), Bermuda grass (*Cynodon dactylon*), and buffalo grass (*Bouteloua dactyloides*), thrive between 25°C (77°F) and 35°C (95°F) and are more drought tolerant. They are hardy, but slow growth or go brown and dormant below 15°C (59°F).

Climate change may mean that gardeners in some areas need to adapt the grass species they grow in order to maintain a healthy lawn and reduce the need for irrigation.

INTRODUCING THE PLANT DIRECTORY

THE DESIGN FOR THE WATERWISE GARDEN CREATES AREAS WITH VERY DIFFERENT GROWING CONDITIONS, FOR EXAMPLE RAISED MOUNDS WITH FREE-DRAINING SOIL AND LOW-LYING DEPRESSIONS WHERE WATER GATHERS. CHOOSING PLANTS TO SUIT THESE CONTRASTING HABITATS IS VITAL FOR THE CREATION OF A RESILIENT PLANTING SCHEME THAT NEEDS MINIMAL WATERING.

The plant directory is arranged under headings for distinct growing conditions, such as plants for crevice gardens and plants for reliably wet areas, and describes a range of plants suited to each habitat, identifying the specific adaptations that allow them to thrive. This list is not definitive, but is intended as a starting point, to help recognize the traits, adaptations, or attributes that make certain plants waterwise choices in the appropriate conditions. Selecting the right plant for the right place is an important first step towards success in any garden, but it is vital for waterwise plantings that need to cope well with their growing conditions with little or no additional watering.

HARDINESS RATINGS

Rating	Temperature ranges	Category
H1a	>15°C (59°F)	Heated greenhouse tropical
H1b	10–15°C (50–59°F)	Heated greenhouse subtropical
H1c	5–10°C (41–50°F)	Heated greenhouse warm temperate
H2	1–5°C (34–41°F)	Cool or frost-free greenhouse
H3	-5–1°C (23–34°F)	Unheated greenhouse/ mild winter
H4	-10– -5°C (14–23°F)	Average winter
H5	-15– -10°C (5–14°F)	Cold winter
H6	-20– -15°C (-4–5°F)	Very cold winter
H7	<-20°C (-4°F)	Very hardy

PLANTING ICONS

Drought-resilient
Plants may have deep root systems, and fleshy/waxy, narrow, or grey, hairy leaves.

Wind-resilient
Plants may have fine or waxy leaves, flexible stems, or branches that won't break easily in high winds.

Plants for pollinators
May have open flowers that offer easy access, or provide a high quantity of nectar and/or pollen.

Resilience to waterlogging
Species that will tolerate periods of waterlogged soil.

RHS Award of Garden Merit
Awarded for excellence, reliability, and performance in UK garden trials.

FRONT GARDEN

Rain garden: fluctuates between wet and dry, depending on rainfall and planting position. Channels in permeable paving: free-draining and sunny. Needs tough, low-growing plants for the driveway.

REAR GARDEN

Crevice gardens: receive full sun and have very free-draining soil. Ephemeral pond: sunken area likely filled with water in winter, but may be dry in summer. Biosolar roof: extremely sunny and exposed.

PLANTS FOR DRY AREAS

PLANTS ADAPTED TO DRY CONDITIONS ARE DROUGHT TOLERANT AND INVALUABLE FOR THEIR ABILITY TO THRIVE IN AREAS WITH FREE-DRAINING SOILS, SUCH AS THE TOP OF ROCKY BANKS AND SUNNY, EXPOSED LOCATIONS, WITHOUT ADDITIONAL WATERING. MANY OF THESE PLANTS DISLIKE WINTER WET, SO NEED GOOD DRAINAGE. THEY ARE BETTER SUITED TO MINERAL MULCHES.

ADAPTATIONS FOR DROUGHT TOLERANCE

- Silvery or grey foliage
- Hairy leaves
- Succulent or fleshy leaves or stems
- Waxy leaves
- Small or narrow leaves
- Aromatic, oily foliage
- Deep or extensive root systems

Drought-tolerant plants thrive in the dry, free-draining soil of sunny banks and berms.

PERENNIALS

Salvia chamaedryoides

This resilient species has silvery leaves that reflect sunlight and are also wax-coated to help reduce evaporation and conserve moisture. A deep root system also enables it to access water in dry conditions. Vibrant blue summer flowers contrast with the silver foliage, attracting pollinators and adding a Mediterranean feel to your planting.

Common name Germander sage
Height/spread 60cm x 60cm (2ft x 2ft) **Foliage** Evergreen
Exposure Full sun **Hardiness** H4

Achillea 'Moonshine'

Flat-topped clusters of small flowers in a vibrant shade of yellow attract pollinators throughout summer and early autumn. Thrives in sunny situations and poor, dry soils thanks to deep roots and silvered, small, feathery foliage, which minimizes water loss.

Common name Yarrow 'Moonshine' **Height/spread** 60cm x 60cm (2ft x 2ft) **Foliage** Semi-evergreen **Exposure** Full sun **Hardiness** H6

Echinops ritro

Tall, silver stems topped with metallic-blue, spherical flowerheads are beloved by bees and butterflies in summer, and make this a dramatic addition to any drought-prone area. Equipped with extensive roots, these large plants are able to access moisture deep in soil. The undersides of the spiky leaves are covered in pale hairs to reduce water loss.

Common name Small globe thistle **Height/spread** 1.2m x 0.5m (48in x 20in) **Foliage** Deciduous **Exposure** Full sun **Hardiness** H7

Verbascum bombyciferum

Huge rosettes of furry, silver leaves give rise to towering spikes of sulphur yellow flowers, which provide striking vertical interest and are a magnet for pollinators. A biennial or short-lived perennial with long taproots that are able to source moisture in dry conditions.

Common name Broussa mullein **Height/spread** 1.8m x 0.6m (6ft x 2ft) **Foliage** Semi-evergreen **Exposure** Full sun **Hardiness** H6

Agapanthus 'Midnight Star'

Drought tolerant, forming clumps of long, strap-like leaves that help minimize moisture loss, and a deep root system, which enables it to access all available moisture from soil layers. Its striking deep blue, globe-like clusters of flowers that appear on tall, slender stems in mid- to late summer add bold form and colour.

Common name African lily 'Midnight Star' **Height/spread** 90cm x 60cm (3ft x 2ft) **Foliage** Evergreen/semi-evergreen **Exposure** Full sun **Hardiness** H5

Centranthus lecoqii

Often found growing out of cracks and gaps in drystone walls and rockeries, the thick roots of this perennial are adept at accessing moisture, while the waxy leaves reduce water loss. Clusters of small, lilac-pink flowers are attractive to pollinators, and give long-lasting colour. *Centranthus ruber* (red valerian) is just as resilient and more commonly available.

Common name Mauve valerian
Height/spread 60cm x 60cm (2ft x 2ft) **Foliage** Evergreen
Exposure Full sun to partial shade
Hardiness H4

Nepeta x *faassenii*

Lavender-blue flowers bloom in spikes during summer at the tips of stems bearing aromatic, grey-green leaves. These blooms are a favourite with many insect pollinators. Aromatic oils in foliage and stems reduce moisture loss and deter pests, but are often attractive to cats.

Common name Catmint
Height/spread 60cm x 60cm (2ft x 2ft) **Foliage** Semi-evergreen
Exposure Full sun **Hardiness** H6

Helleborus argutifolius

Forms impressive clumps of spiny, leathery, dark green leaves and large clusters of pale green flowers from late winter to early spring. Deep roots facilitate access to soil moisture and allow this plant to tolerate dry, semi-shaded conditions.

Common name Holly-leaved hellebore **Height/spread** 1m x 1m (3ft x 3ft) **Foliage** Evergreen
Exposure Partial shade
Hardiness H5

Origanum vulgare

The small, tough leaves minimize water loss and contain aromatic oils to deter pests. Plants form a dense mat that sends up wiry stems tipped with small heads of purple flowers in summer. These are loved by pollinators, and make oregano a great addition to dry herb gardens.

Common name Oregano
Height/spread 50cm x 50cm (20in x 20in) **Foliage** Evergreen
Exposure Full sun to partial shade
Hardiness H6

Hylotelephium spectabile

Thick, fleshy leaves and stems store water, allowing this clump-forming perennial to thrive in dry conditions. Flat heads of small, pink flowers bloom in late summer and turn red in autumn, attracting insect pollinators.

Common name Sedum, ice plant
Height/spread 45cm x 45cm (18in x 18in) **Foliage** Deciduous
Exposure Full sun **Hardiness** H7

Salvia 'Blue Spire' (syn. *Perovskia* 'Blue Spire')

Spikes of lavender-blue flowers are borne on tall stems from late summer into autumn, creating a beautiful contrast with the lacy, silvery-blue, aromatic foliage. These fine, pale leaves are ideally adapted to reduce water loss so that the plant particularly thrives in well-drained and dry conditions.

Common name Russian sage
Height/spread 1.2m x 1m (4ft x 3ft)
Foliage Semi-evergreen **Exposure** Full sun
Hardiness H5

Ceratostigma plumbaginoides

Blue flowers in late summer to early autumn. Small, leathery leaves help minimize water loss and turn red in autumn. Thrives in full sun to partial shade; versatile for dry conditions.

Common name Hardy blue-flowered leadwort
Height/spread 30cm x 30cm (12in x 12in) **Foliage** Deciduous
Exposure Full sun to part shade
Hardiness H5

Tulbaghia violacea

Society garlic form clusters of small, star-shaped, purple flowers in summer, which are attractive to pollinators. Narrow, grey-green leaves help drought tolerance, along with its deep root system. Garlic-scented foliage and flowers deter pests.

Common name Society garlic
Height/spread 45cm x 45cm (18in x 18in)
Foliage Semi-evergreen **Exposure** Full sun to part shade **Hardiness** H3

Oenothera lindheimeri (syn. *Gaura lindheimeri*)

White or pink summer flowers float above long, slender stems, creating a light and airy appearance. Highly drought tolerant due to its deep root system and long, narrow leaves, which reduce water loss.

Common name White gaura, beeblossom
Height/spread 1m x 0.6m (3ft x 2ft)
Foliage Deciduous **Exposure** Full sun
Hardiness H4

GRASSES

Poa labillardierei

This graceful, arching grass has feathery summer flowerheads and soft, blue-green foliage that curls during dry spells to reduce water loss. Its tussock-forming habit conserves soil moisture and its dense, fibrous root system is ideal for stabilizing slopes.

Common name New Zealand blue grass **Height/spread** 1m x 0.8m (3ft x 2.5ft) **Foliage** Semi-evergreen **Exposure** Full sun to part shade **Hardiness** H4

Anemanthele lessoniana

Useful in dry shade under trees, this grass self-seeds prolifically in easier conditions. Elegant coppery leaves create a soft texture, enhanced by airy sprays of red-brown flowerheads in late summer. Leaves curl slightly in dry spells to conserve water.

Common name Pheasant's tail grass **Height/spread** 0.6m x 1m (2ft x 3ft) **Foliage** Evergreen/semi-evergreen **Exposure** Full sun to partial shade **Hardiness** H4

Carex testacea

Striking copper-orange foliage adds year-round colour and texture to gardens. It thrives in well-drained soils thanks to its narrow leaves that help conserve moisture and its dense, fibrous root system, making it ideal for low-maintenance, water-efficient landscapes.

Common name Orange New Zealand sedge **Height/spread** 50cm x 50cm (20in x 20in) **Foliage** Evergreen **Exposure** Full sun to partial shade **Hardiness** H5

Festuca amethystina

Dense clumps of blue-grey foliage turn a soft amethyst hue in the summer, when arching, purple-flushed flowerheads are produced. Fine, needle-like leaves reduce water loss and a deep, fibrous root system allows access to moisture from deeper soil layers. Ideal colour and texture for sunny borders, rock gardens, and low-water landscapes.

Common name Tufted fescue **Height/spread** 60cm x 45cm (24in x 18in) **Foliage** Evergreen **Exposure** Full sun **Hardiness** H5

Stipa pseudoichu

A graceful grass with fine foliage and soft, feathery seedheads that sway in the breeze, providing texture and movement. The narrow leaves minimize water loss and their arching form also helps to conserve moisture by reducing wind exposure. A deep, fibrous root system allows access to moisture from deeper soil layers.

Common name Feather grass
Height/spread 1.5m x 0.45m (5ft x 1½ft) **Foliage** Evergreen
Exposure Full sun **Hardiness** H5

SHRUBS

Teucrium fruticans

Small leaves coated in tiny silvery hairs reflect sunlight and help the plant retain moisture. Pretty pale blue flowers adorn this drought-tolerant shrub in summer and are popular with pollinators.

Common name Tree germander
Height/spread 1.5m x 1.5m (5ft x 5ft)
Foliage Evergreen **Exposure** Full sun
Hardiness H3

Phlomis purpurea

Grey, woolly leaves and stems reduce moisture loss and add texture to dry gardens. The deep roots can access moisture in stony soil. Whorls of hooked, lilac-pink flowers appear on the upright stems in summer and are attractive to pollinators. *Phlomis fruticosa* is a hardier, yellow-flowered option.

Common name Purple Jerusalem sage
Height/spread 1.5m x 1.5m (5ft x 5ft)
Foliage Evergreen **Exposure** Full sun
Hardiness H4

Elaeagnus 'Quicksilver'

A large shrub, with bright, silvery, hairy foliage that reflects sunlight and reduces water loss. A robust root system maximizes moisture uptake in dry soils and also fixes nitrogen to fuel growth. Small, fragrant, yellow flowers in summer are followed by autumn berries.

Common name Oleaster 'Quicksilver'
Height/spread 3m x 3m (10ft x 10ft)
Foliage Deciduous **Exposure** Full sun
Hardiness H5

TREES

Cistus × *purpureus*

Highly drought tolerant due to its narrow, resinous, aromatic leaves, which help reduce moisture loss during transpiration. Large, vibrant purple-pink flowers bloom in early summer and attract many pollinators. An extensive root system allows these shrubs to access available water from poor soils.

Common name Purple-flowered rock rose
Height/spread 1.2m × 1m (4ft × 3ft)
Foliage Evergreen **Exposure** Full sun
Hardiness H4

Punica granatum

Known for its striking orange-red flowers and vibrant, edible fruit, the pomegranate thrives in hot Mediterranean climates. The small, thick, leathery leaves help minimize water loss and its deep root system allows it to access water from lower soil layers.

Common name Pomegranate
Height/spread 5m × 4m (15ft × 12ft)
Foliage Deciduous **Exposure** Full sun
Hardiness H3

Lavandula × *intermedia* 'Grosso'

A large lavender variety with fine, aromatic, silver foliage to reduce water loss. Tall spikes of fragrant, deep purple, summer flowers are a magnet for pollinators. Ideal for ornamental and culinary uses.

Common name Lavender 'Grosso'
Height/spread 90cm × 90cm (3ft × 3ft)
Foliage Evergreen **Exposure** Full sun
Hardiness H5

Arbutus andrachne

A striking, evergreen tree with white, bell-shaped flowers in spring, followed by small, strawberry-like, red fruit in autumn. Its attractive red-brown bark peels to shed damaged layers, protecting the tree from intense sunlight, and glossy, leathery foliage minimizes water loss.

Common name Grecian strawberry tree
Height/spread 10m × 5m (30ft × 15ft)
Foliage Evergreen **Exposure** Full sun
Hardiness H4

PLANTS FOR
CREVICE GARDENS

WITH LIMITED SOIL DEPTH, SHARP DRAINAGE, AND FULL EXPOSURE TO SUNLIGHT, CREVICE GARDENS PRESENT CHALLENGING CONDITIONS FOR PLANTS (SEE P.123). THOSE THAT FLOURISH ORIGINATE FROM TOUGH ALPINE OR COASTAL HABITATS, AND HAVE COMPACT FORMS ADAPTED TO CONSERVE MOISTURE, AS WELL AS SURPRISINGLY BEAUTIFUL FLOWERS.

ADAPTATIONS OF CREVICE GARDEN PLANTS

- Small, compact form
- Succulent or waxy leaves
- Small or narrow leaves
- Aromatic foliage
- Deep root systems
- Summer dormancy

[Above] A crevice garden makes an ideal home for low-growing alpine and succulent plants.

Saxifraga paniculata

This compact, evergreen perennial forms tight, low rosettes of small, narrow leaves that reduce the plant's surface area and are ideally adapted to conserve moisture. Delicate sprays of white or pink flowers are borne on slender stems from late spring to early summer.
Common name Lifelong saxifrage
Height/spread 20cm x 30cm (8in x 12in)
Foliage Evergreen **Exposure** Full sun to part shade **Hardiness** H5

Pulsatilla vulgaris

A striking perennial with finely divided leaves, and large, bell-shaped purple or white flowers in early spring, followed by feathery seed heads. Ideal for crevice gardens, rockeries, or dry borders, where its deep roots help it access moisture.

Common name Pasque flower
Height/spread 30cm x 30cm (12in x 12in) **Foliage** Deciduous
Exposure Full sun **Hardiness** H5

Sempervivum tectorum

This hardy succulent stores water in its green, red, or purple rosettes of fleshy leaves, allowing it to withstand drought. Rosettes form offsets (chicks) that allow plants to spread naturally. In late summer some rosettes form thick stems carrying small, star-shaped flowers.

Common name Common houseleek, hens and chicks
Height/spread 15cm x 30cm (6in x 12in) **Foliage** Evergreen
Exposure Full sun **Hardiness** H6

Thymus serpyllum

Aromatic, with tiny, green leaves, this low-growing thyme is well adapted to dry conditions and forms dense mats that act as ground cover, reducing moisture loss. Plants are covered in small purple flowers in late spring to early summer, attracting many pollinators.

Common name Wild thyme, creeping thyme
Height/spread 10cm x 30cm (4in x 12in) **Foliage** Evergreen
Exposure Full sun **Hardiness** H5

Iberis sempervirens

A mound of narrow, leathery leaves minimizes water loss. Bears clusters of white spring flowers.

Common name Perennial candytuft
Height/spread 30cm x 45cm (12in x 18in)
Foliage Evergreen **Exposure** Full sun
Hardiness H5

Dianthus deltoides

Low-growing, with narrow, green leaves that conserve water and many pink flowers in summer.

Common name Maiden pink
Height/spread 15cm x 30cm (6in x 12in)
Foliage Evergreen **Exposure** Full sun
Hardiness H6

Draba aizoides

A tiny, low-growing alpine with small, narrow leaves to reduce water loss, and a compact form to help it withstand harsh conditions. Bears clusters of vibrant yellow flowers in spring.

Common name Yellow whitlow grass
Height/spread 10cm x 20cm (4in x 8in)
Foliage Evergreen **Exposure** Full sun
Hardiness H5

Eriogonum umbellatum

Mats of grey-green leaves, with wooly undersides, are well adapted to minimize water loss. A deep root system gives good access to soil moisture. Clusters of tiny, bright yellow flowers are borne in summer and fade to copper.

Common name Sulphur flower
Height/spread 30cm x 60cm (1ft x 2ft)
Foliage Evergreen **Exposure** Full sun
Hardiness H4

Armeria maritima

A drought- and salt-tolerant coastal plant. Dense clumps of thin, leathery, evergreen leaves minimize water loss. Pink flowers top stiff stems in late spring and summer.

Common name Thrift, sea pink
Height/spread 20cm x 30cm (8in x 12in)
Foliage Evergreen **Exposure** Full sun
Hardiness H5

Alyssum montanum

A low-growing perennial with small, hairy, grey-green foliage that is well adapted to retain moisture. Fragrant, bright yellow flowers appear on long stems in late spring and early summer.

Common name Basket of gold
Height/spread 30cm x 50cm (12in x 20in)
Foliage Evergreen **Exposure** Full sun
Hardiness H6

Lewisia cotyledon

Rosettes of long, green, fleshy leaves enable this plant to store water, making it drought tolerant. Produces clusters of vibrant flowers in shades of pink, white, or orange, on long stems. Protect from winter wet.

Common name Siskiyou lewisia
Height/spread 30cm x 30cm (12in x 12in)
Foliage Evergreen **Exposure** Full sun to partial shade **Hardiness** H4

Veronica prostrata

Forms a dense, low-growing mat of small, narrow, green leaves that conserves moisture and is ideal for ground cover, between paving, or low-maintenance lawns. Produces spikes of small, blue flowers in late spring and early summer.

Common name Prostrate speedwell
Height/spread 15cm x 45cm (6in x 18in)
Foliage Evergreen **Exposure** Full sun to part shade **Hardiness** H5

Tulipa humilis 'Eastern Star'

This dwarf tulip stores moisture in its bulb and has grey-green leaves, allowing it to survive extended dry periods. The striking purple flowers, with yellow centres, appear in early spring.

Common name Tulip 'Eastern Star'
Height/spread 15cm x 15cm (6in x 6in)
Foliage Deciduous **Exposure** Full sun
Hardiness H5

Bulbine frutescens

An attractive perennial with long, fleshy leaves that store water. Produces long spires of small, star-shaped, orange or yellow flowers in summer, which attract pollinators.

Common name Stalked bulbine
Height/spread 40cm x 90cm (16in x 36in)
Foliage Evergreen **Exposure** Full sun
Hardiness H3

WATERWISE PLANTING

PLANTS FOR
RAIN GARDENS AND TEMPORARILY WET AREAS

> **ADAPTATIONS FOR PLANTS IN TEMPORARILY WET AREAS**
>
> - Dense root systems
> - Glossy, leathery leaves
> - Swollen roots or underground storage organs
> - Adventitious roots

RAIN GARDENS, SWALES, EPHEMERAL PONDS, AND DAMP DEPRESSIONS CAPTURE RAINWATER RUNOFF AND CREATE TEMPORARY POOLS. THEIR PLANTING MUST BE ABLE TO TOLERATE FLUCTUATING MOISTURE LEVELS, AS WATER DRAINS AWAY DURING DRY PERIODS.

Rain garden planting can be inspired by similar habitats, such as ephemeral ponds or wetlands.

PERENNIALS

Rudbeckia triloba 'Prairie Glow'

A short-lived perennial, with basal leaves and stiff stems supporting bright orange-yellow, daisy-like flowers with a striking dark centre in late summer. Tolerates wet soils and thrives in fluctuating moisture levels.

Common name Brown-eyed Susan
Height/spread 80cm x 60cm (32in x 24in) **Foliage** Deciduous
Exposure Full sun **Hardiness** H6

Crocosmia 'Lucifer'

Bold red flowers emerge in mid- to late summer from upright stands of tall, sword-shaped foliage, creating dramatic displays. Forms underground corms that store water and nutrients, aiding drought survival.

Common name Montbretia 'Lucifer' **Height/spread** 1m x 0.6m (3ft x 2ft) **Foliage** Deciduous **Exposure** Full sun to partial shade **Hardiness** H5

Eupatorium maculatum Atropurpureum Group

A tall perennial that bears terminal clusters of pink flowers on upright stems from late summer into autumn. Loved by insect pollinators. Thrives in moist and waterlogged soils, and the strong stems resist flood damage.

Common name Joe-Pye weed **Height/spread** 2.2m x 1m (7ft x 3ft) **Foliage** Deciduous **Exposure** Full sun to partial shade **Hardiness** H7

Iris sibirica

Slender, grass-like leaves and blue, early summer flowers borne on tall stems, make this a standout plant for moist areas. Thick, rhizomatous roots give it tolerance of both waterlogging and drought.

Common name Siberian iris **Height/spread** 90cm x 60cm (3ft x 2ft) **Foliage** Deciduous **Exposure** Full sun to part shade **Hardiness** H7

Hemerocallis lilioasphodelus

Hardy perennials with arching foliage and a succession of vibrant, trumpet-shaped, summer blooms that last a single day. Moisture is stored in the fleshy roots, allowing daylilies to thrive in variable moisture levels.

Common name Yellow daylily **Height/spread** 90cm x 60cm (3ft x 2ft) **Foliage** Deciduous **Exposure** Full sun to partial shade **Hardiness** H6

Rheum palmatum

Deeply lobed green or red-tinged foliage can reach an impressive size. From late spring to early summer, towering flower spikes with pink-red blooms add vertical interest. Its robust roots and rhizomes are adapted to maximize access to soil water.

Common name Chinese rhubarb **Height/spread** 2m x 1.5m (6ft x5ft) **Foliage** Deciduous **Exposure** Full sun to partial shade **Hardiness** H6

Filipendula ulmaria

Ideal for damp borders or meadows, this wetland species copes with dry spells well by reducing growth. Creates clumps of divided, green leaves with elegant frothy, cream flowerheads in midsummer.

Common name Meadowsweet
Height/spread 1.2m x 0.6m (4ft x 2ft) **Foliage** Deciduous
Exposure Full sun to part shade
Hardiness H6

Iris chrysographes

Dramatic black-purple, early summer flowers add elegance above narrow, grey-green foliage. Ideal for damp, sunny borders because the fleshy rhizomes tolerate waterlogging and contain stores for drought recovery.

Common name Black iris
Height/spread 80cm x 60cm (32in x 30in) **Foliage** Deciduous
Exposure Full sun to part shade
Hardiness H6

Lythrum salicaria

Tall, upright stems with willow-like foliage carry attractive spikes of pink-purple flowers in summer, which are loved by pollinators. Prefers damp or boggy soils, but the extensive root system provides drought resistance.

Common name Purple loosestrife
Height/spread 1.2m x 0.6m (4ft x 2ft) **Foliage** Deciduous
Exposure Full sun **Hardiness** H7

Sanguisorba officinalis

Tall spikes of red, bottlebrush-like flowers add colour above clumps of pinnate leaves. Thick, rhizomatous roots help the plant access and retain moisture in drier areas, but cope well with wet conditions.

Common name Great burnet
Height/spread 1m x 0.6m (3ft x 2ft)
Foliage Deciduous
Exposure Full sun to partial shade
Hardiness H7

GRASSES

Camassia leichtlinii

Long, elegant stems carry showy blue or white star-like flowers in late spring, above basal clumps of strap-like leaves. The bulbs of this perennial prefer moist soil, making it ideal for damp meadows, but also enable its survival through dry periods.

Common name Camassia **Height/spread** 80cm x 30cm (32in x 12in) **Foliage** Deciduous **Exposure** Full sun to partial shade **Hardiness** H4

Carex remota

A tough, clump-forming sedge with slender, arching foliage and small yellow-green flowers in summer. Tolerates waterlogged soil. Fibrous roots stabilize soil and improve water infiltration.

Common name Remote sedge **Height/spread** 50cm x 50cm (20in x 20in) **Foliage** Evergreen **Exposure** Full sun to partial shade **Hardiness** H5

Lysimachia punctata

A tough plant that thrives in boggy conditions or standing water, but can be invasive if conditions are too wet, making it a better choice for a rain garden. Upright stems produce bell-shaped, yellow flowers in midsummer, which are attractive to pollinators.

Common name Dotted loosestrife **Height/spread** 1m x 0.6m (3ft x 2ft) **Foliage** Deciduous **Exposure** Full sun to partial shade **Hardiness** H6

Deschampsia cespitosa

This graceful grass forms tussocks of dark green leaves. Its tall arching stems bear, silvered, feathery flowerheads. Ideal for naturalistic plantings, it thrives in damp conditions but can withstand drought due to its deep root system.

Common name Tufted hair grass **Height/spread** 1m x 0.6m (3ft x 2ft) **Foliage** Evergreen **Exposure** Full sun to partial shade **Hardiness** H6

Carex morrowii 'Irish Green'

A useful perennial sedge that forms tidy, evergreen clumps of arching, bright green leaves. Pale flower spikes are borne on upright stems in summer. Tolerant of wet soil, these plants can also cope well with temporary dryness.

Common name Morrow's sedge 'Irish Green'
Height/spread 45cm x 50cm (18in x 20in) **Foliage** Evergreen
Exposure Full sun to partial shade
Hardiness H7

Calamagrostis brachytricha

Compact, with a neat clump of arching grey-green leaves and a mass of upright, plumed flowerheads in summer. Tolerates damp soil well and survives drought with dormancy.

Common name Korean feather reed grass
Height/spread 1.2m x 0.6m (4ft x 2ft) **Foliage** Deciduous
Exposure Full sun to partial shade
Hardiness H6

Molinia caerulea

An upright grass, forming clumps of bright green foliage with attractive autumn colour and airy flowerheads. Perfect for meadow-style planting, it is a native of wetlands that survives drought with a dormant root system.

Common name Purple moor grass
Height/spread 1m x 1m (3ft x 3ft)
Foliage Deciduous
Exposure Full sun to partial shade
Hardiness H7

Miscanthus sinensis

Spectacular ornamental grass with tall, upright stems bearing arching leaves and dramatic plumes of flowerheads in late summer; ideal for structural impact. Thrives in wet soils and withstands dry periods thanks to water storage in thick rhizomes. Many cultivars are also available.

Common name Eulalia
Height/spread 2m x 1.5m (6ft x 5ft) **Foliage** Deciduous
Exposure Full sun **Hardiness** H6

SHRUBS

Salix purpurea

This vigorous shrub has slender, purplish stems and narrow, blue-green foliage. It produces small, silvery catkins in spring, before leaves emerge. Thrives in wet soil, with long roots that stabilize damp ground and access deep water reserves during dry spells.

Common name Purple willow **Height/spread** 3m x 2m (10ft x 6ft) **Foliage** Deciduous **Exposure** Full sun **Hardiness** H6

Cornus sanguinea

An attractive shrub with vibrant red young stems in winter, white spring flowers followed by dark berries, and green leaves that fade to red in autumn. Grows well in damp soil and tolerates waterlogging by producing adventitious roots.

Common name Common dogwood **Height/spread** 3m x 2.5m (10ft x 8ft) **Foliage** Deciduous **Exposure** Full sun to partial shade **Hardiness** H6

Viburnum opulus

Perfect for wildlife gardens, this large shrub has dense, flat clusters of white flowers in late spring and early summer, followed by vibrant red berries. Native to damp areas, it resists drought using its deep root system.

Common name Guelder rose **Height/spread** 4m x 2.5m (13ft x 8ft) **Foliage** Deciduous **Exposure** Full sun to partial shade **Hardiness** H6

Rosa rugosa

A robust, hardy shrub with fragrant pink or white flowers from summer to autumn, and then clusters of large, red hips. Tolerates challenging soils, including wet and saline conditions. Retains water in thick, thorny stems and tough, glossy leaves.

Common name Japanese rose
Height/spread 1.5m x 1.5m (5ft x 5ft) **Foliage** Deciduous
Exposure Full sun
Hardiness H7

Sambucus nigra

This multi-stemmed shrub has fragrant, creamy flowerheads in late spring, and large clusters of black fruits. Useful in hedgerows or wildlife gardens, it thrives in moist soils, where its deep roots tolerate both waterlogging and dry conditions.

Common name Common elder
Height/spread 6m x 6m (20ft x 20ft) **Foliage** Deciduous
Exposure Full sun to partial shade
Hardiness H6

Aronia melanocarpa

A compact, bushy shrub with attractive white late spring flowers, glossy green leaves, and black fruits. It is very hardy and suitable for sites with boggy conditions, but is also capable of tolerating dry spells.

Common name Black chokeberry
Height/spread 2m x 2m (6ft x 6ft)
Foliage Deciduous
Exposure Full sun to partial shade
Hardiness H7

Hydrangea quercifolia

An elegant shrub with oak-shaped leaves that turn vibrant shades in autumn. The conical white flowerheads are borne in summer then fade to pink. It enjoys moist, well-drained soils, where it will tolerate periods of wetness and cope with full sun. In drier soils plant in partial shade.

Common name Oak-leaved hydrangea **Height/spread** 2m x 2m (6ft x 6ft) **Foliage** Deciduous
Exposure Full sun to partial shade
Hardiness H5

GROUND COVER

Ajuga reptans

This low-growing perennial has dark, bronze-purple foliage and spikes of blue flowers that are attractive to pollinators. It is ideal ground cover in damp areas, but also tolerates periods of dryness well.

Common name Bugle **Height/spread** 20cm x 1m (8in x 40in) **Foliage** Evergreen **Exposure** Full sun to part shade **Hardiness** H7

Lysimachia nummularia

Vigorous ground cover that thrives in wet soil, producing trailing stems with adventitious roots and attractive, rounded leaves. Bright yellow flowers appear in summer. May suffer in drought, but regrows quickly.

Common name Creeping Jenny **Height/spread** 10cm x 50cm (4in x 20in) **Foliage** Evergreen **Exposure** Full sun to part shade **Hardiness** H6

Bistorta affinis (syn. Persicaria affinis)

This mat-forming plant produces small, glossy green leaves that turn bronze in winter. Spikes of pink flowers emerge from midsummer into autumn. Prefers moist soil, but will cope in dry conditions.

Common name Lesser knotweed **Height/spread** 30cm x 60cm (12in x 24in) **Foliage** Semi-evergreen **Exposure** Full sun to part shade **Hardiness** H6

Waldsteinia ternata

Attractive dense, spreading growth of three-lobed, strawberry-like leaves. It bears yellow flowers in spring and summer. Thick, rhizomatous roots can withstand both wet and dry soil.

Common name Siberian waldsteinia **Height/spread** 20cm x 1m (8in x 40in) **Foliage** Semi-evergreen **Exposure** Full sun to full shade **Hardiness** H7

FERNS

Matteuccia struthiopteris

A large, vase-shaped fern, with thick rhizomatous roots that thrive in moist and waterlogged soils, making it ideal for a damp woodland garden. Fronds brown and collapse in dry conditions, but plants may regrow from rhizomes once moisture returns.

Common Name Shuttlecock fern, ostrich fern
Height/spread 1.5m x 1m (5ft x 3ft)
Foliage Deciduous **Exposure** Partial to full shade **Hardiness** H5

Dryopteris filix-mas

This tough, vigorous fern unfurls arching fronds from the crown of brown rhizomes at its base. Its robust rhizomes allow it to cope with moisture fluctuations, but it thrives in moist, shaded borders.

Common Name Male fern
Height/spread 1m x 0.6m (3ft x 2ft)
Foliage Deciduous **Exposure** Partial to full shade **Hardiness** H7

Athyrium filix-femina

Elegant, with very delicate, finely divided fronds, this deciduous fern is particularly tolerant of shade and moist soils. Its basal rhizomes allow it to withstand temporary dry spells.

Common Name Lady fern
Height/spread 1m x 0.5m (3ft x 20in)
Foliage Deciduous
Exposure Partial to full shade
Hardiness H6

TREES

Betula nigra

Known for its striking, peeling bark in shades of cinnamon, cream, and grey, as well as butter yellow autumn foliage, this tree adds year-round interest. It thrives in poorly drained soils thanks to tough, water-resistant bark and resilient roots, which are also tolerant of dry spells.

Common name Black birch
Height/spread 15m x 10m (50ft x 30ft) **Foliage** Deciduous
Exposure Full sun to part shade
Hardiness H7

Acer campestre

A compact tree, native to the UK, with vibrant autumn foliage and winged fruits; ideal for hedgerows or gardens. Prefers a moist, well-drained soil, but its adaptable root system can cope with periods of wet or dry.

Common Name Field maple
Height/spread 12m x 7m (40ft x 22ft) **Foliage** Deciduous
Exposure Full sun to part shade
Hardiness H6

Alnus glutinosa

Prefers a sunny location and wet or waterlogged areas, and grows well in poor soils thanks to nitrogen-fixing nodules on its roots. Often used to stabilize wet ground. An attractive tree with leathery, lobed leaves and catkins in late winter or early spring.

Common Name Common Alder
Height/spread 20m x 8m (70ft x 26ft) **Foliage** Deciduous
Exposure Full sun to part shade
Hardiness H7

Cercis canadensis

A beautiful tree with pink flowers on bare stems in spring and heart-shaped leaves with good autumn colour. Thrives in damp soil, but tolerates drought.

Common Name Eastern redbud
Height/spread 10m x 8m (30ft x 26ft)
Foliage Deciduous **Exposure** Full sun to part shade **Hardiness** H5

Salix alba

A fast-growing tree with silvery foliage, ideal for wet landscapes. It can be pollarded to limit its size. Loves wet ground, but also drought-resistant.

Common Name White willow
Height/spread 25m x 15m (80ft x 50ft)
Foliage Deciduous **Exposure** Full sun
Hardiness H6

WATERWISE PLANTING

> ### ADAPTATIONS FOR WET AREAS
>
> - Dense root systems
> - Shallow roots
> - Glossy, leathery leaves
> - Swollen roots or underground storage organs
> - Adventitious roots

Plants adapted to wet areas provide valuable habitat and food for a range of aquatic and semi-aquatic wildlife.

PLANTS FOR
RELIABLY WET AREAS

FOR AREAS THAT REMAIN WET IN DEEPER PARTS OF EPHEMERAL PONDS OR BOG GARDENS, IT'S VITAL TO CHOOSE PLANTS THAT ARE ADAPTED TO GROW IN THE LOW-OXYGEN CONDITIONS FOUND IN WATERLOGGED OR SUBMERGED SOIL. BE SURE THAT THE AREA WILL REMAIN WET, BECAUSE THESE PLANTS WILL STRUGGLE, OR EVEN DIE, IN DRY SOIL.

Astilbe rivularis

Prized for its bold mounds of divided foliage and tall plumes of white flowers in summer, this astilbe thrives in streamsides or pond edges thanks to a fibrous root system. *Astilbe* x *arendsii* hybrids also suit these conditions.

Common name Waterside astilbe
Height/spread 1m x 0.6m (3ft x 2ft)
Foliage Deciduous **Exposure** Partial shade to full shade **Hardiness** H4

Alisma plantago-aquatica

Adapted to shallow water or pond margins, this perennial has broad grey-green leaves that float on the water's surface and a fibrous root system for anchorage in wet soils. Tall sprays of white or pink, star-shaped flowers are produced in late spring.

Common name Water plantain
Height/spread 50cm x 30cm (20in x 12in)
Foliage Deciduous **Exposure** Full sun to part shade **Hardiness** H7

Butomus umbellatus

With rush-like leaves and upright stems bearing umbrella-shaped clusters of pink flowers in summer, this perennial is well adapted to shallow water. Deep, spreading roots anchor it in wet soils at the edges of ponds or wetland areas.

Common name Flowering rush
Height/spread 1.2m x 0.6m (4ft x 2ft)
Foliage Deciduous **Exposure** Full sun
Hardiness H5

Calla palustris

The dramatic contrast of the large, white flower spathes and central yellow spadices against the glossy, green, heart-shaped foliage makes the water arum an excellent choice for wetland gardens. It blooms from late spring to summer. Spreading rhizomes are well adapted to waterlogged conditions.

Common name Water arum
Height/spread 30cm x 30cm (12in x 12in) **Foliage** Deciduous
Exposure Full shade **Hardiness** H7

Caltha palustris

Large, rounded, waxy leaves are held on long, sturdy stems to prevent excess water absorption, while the root system can tolerate persistently wet or submerged conditions at pond margins. Bright golden-yellow flowers bloom above the foliage in early spring and are attractive to polllinators.

Common name Marsh marigold
Height/spread 30cm x 40cm (12in x 16in) **Foliage** Deciduous
Exposure Full sun **Hardiness** H7

Carex elata 'Aurea'

This perennial sedge forms a dense clump of golden, grass-like foliage, with small brown flower spikes in early summer. It thrives in wet or poorly drained areas and its root system stabilizes wet soils and helps to absorb excess moisture.

Common name Bowles's golden sedge
Height/spread 60cm x 60cm (2ft x 2ft) **Foliage** Evergreen
Exposure Full sun to partial shade
Hardiness H6

Cyperus giganteus

This papyrus adds an architectural element to ponds and other aquatic landscapes, where it can survive frost if its crown is underwater. Its tall, flexible stems are topped by delicate, umbrella-shaped foliage. Thick rhizomes and a robust root system anchor it in soft, wet soil.

Common name Mexican papyrus
Height/spread 2m x 1m (6ft x 3ft)
Foliage Evergreen **Exposure** Full sun
Hardiness H4

Equisetum hyemale

This horsetail has hollow, vertical stems, with dark bands at their joints, that are perfectly adapted to standing water. It thrives in poorly drained soils, spreading via rhizomes. Ideal to create vertical interest in boggy areas or pond margins, but often grown in containers to prevent its spread.

Common name Rough horsetail
Height/spread 1.5m x 0.6m (5ft x 2ft)
Foliage Evergreen **Exposure** Full sun to part shade **Hardiness** H7

Filipendula rubra 'Venusta'

This striking perennial bears tall, airy plumes of soft pink summer flowers, above deeply divided, fern-like leaves, adding texture to water-edge planting. It thrives in moist or wet conditions, where its rhizomes and fibrous roots stabilize soft soils. May be invasive in optimum conditions.

Common name Meadowsweet 'Venusta'
Height/spread 2m x 1.2m (6ft x 4ft)
Foliage Deciduous **Exposure** Full sun to partial shade **Hardiness** H5

Houttuynia cordata

A creeping perennial with blue-green foliage and small white flowers in spring. Perfect for ground cover in wetland areas or pond margins. Its rhizomes are well adapted to wet conditions, where they spread aggressively.

Common name Heart-leaved houttuynia
Height/spread 30cm x 50cm (12in x 20in)
Foliage Deciduous **Exposure** Full sun to part shade **Hardiness** H6

Iris laevigata

Thrives in wet soils and shallow water, where thick rhizomes anchor the plant and erect, waxy leaves prevent moisture absorption when submerged. Large purple flowers with white flashes on the fall petals are produced from late spring into summer.

Common name Smooth iris
Height/spread 70cm x 50cm (28in x 20in)
Foliage Deciduous **Exposure** Full sun
Hardiness H6

Juncus effusus

Forms grass-like clumps of evergreen, tubular, arching stems with rounded green to brown flowerheads emerging just below the tips from spring into summer. Perfect vertical structure for wet areas. Its fibrous roots help stabilize the soil.

Common name Common rush, soft rush
Height/spread 1.2m x 0.6m (4ft x 2ft)
Foliage Evergreen **Exposure** Full sun to part shade **Hardiness** H6

Lobelia cardinalis

This perennial forms clumps of bright green leaves that produce upright stems bearing brilliant red flowers from summer into autumn. Its shallow root system secures the plant while being able to access oxygen. Ideal for bog gardens.

Common name Cardinal flower
Height/spread 1m x 0.45m (3ft x 1½ft)
Foliage Deciduous **Exposure** Full sun to part shade **Hardiness** H3

Osmunda cinnamomea

Forms an elegant upright clump of green sterile fronds that contrast beautifully with cinnamon-coloured fertile fronds in spring. Well adapted to wet, acidic soils with a fibrous root system for anchorage and fronds that shed water efficiently, avoiding fungal infections.

Common name Cinnamon fern
Height/spread 1m x 0.6m (3ft x 2ft) **Foliage** Deciduous
Exposure Partial to full shade
Hardiness H6

Primula beesiana

This spectacular addition to damp gardens has low rosettes of light green foliage that give rise to upright stems bearing tiered whorls of magenta to deep-pink flowers through late spring and early summer. Its fibrous root system thrives in damp, humus-rich soils.

Common name Bee's primrose
Height/spread 60cm x 30cm (2ft x 1ft) **Foliage** Deciduous
Exposure Partial shade
Hardiness H6

Menyanthes trifoliata

This plant is adapted to grow in shallow water, where its distinctive leaves – made up of three leaflets – are held above the water on floating, spreading stems, along with clusters of white summer flowers that are popular with pollinators. Its extensive rhizomatous root system effectively absorbs and stores nutrients from submerged soils.

Common name Bogbean
Height/spread 0.30m x 1m (1ft x 3ft) **Foliage** Deciduous
Exposure Full sun to part shade
Hardiness H7

Myosotis scorpioides

This perennial thrives in wet soil or shallow water thanks to a rhizomatous root system that helps it absorb and store nutrients. Spreading mounds of narrow, green leaves are covered in clusters of tiny, sky blue flowers through late spring and summer.

Common name Water forget-me-not
Height/spread 30cm x 30cm (12in x 12in) **Foliage** Deciduous
Exposure Full sun to part shade
Hardiness H6

Thelypteris palustris

A delicate, deciduous fern with upright, feathery, sometimes twisted fronds. It thrives in wet, acidic soils, which makes it ideal for wet woodland gardens. Creeping rhizomes and fibrous roots anchor plants firmly in soft, wet soils.

Common name Marsh fern
Height/spread 1m x 0.45m (3ft x 1½ft) **Foliage** Deciduous
Exposure Partial to full shade
Hardiness H6

Geum rivale

This perennial's airy clusters of nodding, bell-shaped flowers come in shades of pink, red, or yellow, and appear from spring to midsummer. The spreading rhizomes and fibrous roots stabilize moist soil, and can tolerate waterlogging and even occasional flooding.

Common name Water avens
Height/spread 60cm x 50cm (24in x 20in) **Foliage** Deciduous
Exposure Full sun to part shade
Hardiness H7

Schoenoplectus lacustris subsp. *tabernaemontani*

With its elegant, upright, grey-green stems and soft, cylindrical flower spikes, the grey club-rush is a graceful addition to naturalistic damp gardens. Its growth is less vigorous than other rushes, but may still need management in smaller ponds. Spreading rhizomes and fibrous roots stabilize moist soils.

Common name Grey club-rush
Height/spread 1.2m x 0.6m (4ft x 2ft)
Foliage Evergreen **Exposure** Full sun to partial shade **Hardiness** H7

Bistorta officinalis (syn. *Persicaria bistorta*)

Common bistort's broad, green leaves create lush ground cover, protecting soil beneath. Spires of soft-pink flowers are borne on erect stems in early summer. Its robust rhizomes colonize wet ground, tolerating seasonal flooding and waterlogging.

Common name Common bistort
Height/spread 1m x 0.6m (3ft x 2ft)
Foliage Deciduous or semi evergreen
Exposure Full sun to part shade **Hardiness** H7

Primula vialii

This perennial produces unusual and striking red and purple flower spikes, reminiscent of orchids, on tall stems above rosettes of pale green foliage. Perfect for wet areas and bogs, it loves consistently moist or waterlogged conditions, where its fibrous root system effectively absorbs nutrients.

Common name Vial's primrose
Height/spread 30cm x 30cm (12in x 12in)
Foliage Deciduous **Exposure** Partial shade
Hardiness H5

Ranunculus flammula

Ideal for the edges of ponds, bogs, and streams this small marginal aquatic perennial produces creeping stems with spear-shaped leaves and many yellow flowers in summer. Roots form along the stems helping the plant cope with waterlogged soil.

Common name Lesser spearwort
Height/spread 30cm x 30cm (12in x 12in)
Foliage Deciduous **Exposure** Full sun
Hardiness H7

Ranunculus acris

This perennial bears showy, yellow flowers in late spring and early summer, above bright green, lobed leaves; perfect to brighten up damp, grassy meadows or other moist areas. Its fibrous root system thrives in waterlogged or clay-rich soils, and can withstand seasonal flooding.

Common name Meadow buttercup
Height/spread 60cm x 30cm
(24in x 12in) **Foliage** Deciduous
Exposure Full sun to partial shade
Hardiness H7

Sagittaria sagittifolia

Arrowhead is a perennial adapted to growing in shallow water or very waterlogged soils, where its arrow-shaped leaves float to capture sunlight and its roots absorb nutrients from water. It produces white flowers in summer.

Common name Arrowhead
Height/spread 1m x 0.6m
(3ft x 2ft) **Foliage** Deciduous
Exposure Full sun **Hardiness** H6

Typha minima

This smaller species of bulrush adds vertical structure to wetland gardens with its slender grass-like leaves and cylindrical flowerheads. Less invasive than larger bulrushes, its spreading rhizomes and flexible stems allow it to thrive in shallow water.

Common name Dwarf bulrush
Height/spread 60cm x 30cm
(2ft x 1ft) **Foliage** Deciduous
Exposure Full sun **Hardiness** H6

Zantedeschia aethiopica

At home in wet soils or shallow pond margins, the arum lily has large rhizomes that can tolerate constantly wet conditions and store nutrients. Its glossy, deep green leaves are the perfect foil for the elegant white flowers with yellow spadices at their centres.

Common name Arum lily
Height/spread 1m x 0.6m
(3ft x 2ft) **Foliage** Evergreen or semi-evergreen
Exposure Full sun to partial shade
Hardiness H4

PLANTS FOR
WATERWISE LAWNS

THESE PLANTS ARE SPLIT INTO TWO CATEGORIES; THOSE THAT CAN BE ADDED TO TRADITIONAL GRASS LAWNS TO INCREASE RESILIENCE TO DROUGHT, AND LOW-GROWING, GROUND COVER PLANTS THAT CAN BE USED TO REPLACE GRASS LAWNS ENTIRELY. ALL OF THESE TOUGH PLANTS ARE ABLE TO TOLERATE SOME FOOT TRAFFIC AND, UNLIKE GRASS, WILL STAY GREEN IN HOT SUMMER WEATHER.

> ### ADAPTATIONS OF PLANTS FOR WATERWISE LAWNS
>
> - Small or narrow leaves
> - Aromatic foliage
> - Low-growing, compact form
> - Deep root systems

Trifolium repens (white clover) and *Prunella vulgaris* (self heal) add colour, resilience, and valuable nectar sources for pollinators to a lawn.

ADDITIONS TO GRASS LAWNS

Achillea millefolium

A spreading, drought-tolerant perennial with narrow, feathery foliage that reduces water loss and stays green in drought conditions. Flat-topped heads of small flowers, in colours ranging from white to pink, are produced in summer and are attractive to pollinators.

Common name Common yarrow
Height/spread 60cm x 60cm (2ft x 2ft) **Foliage** Deciduous
Exposure Full sun **Hardiness** H7

Trifolium repens

A low-growing, creeping perennial that roots at the nodes along its stems, and has nitrogen-fixing root nodules, both of which help it to remain green in dry conditions and on poor soils. White flowers bloom in late spring and summer, and are a magnet for bees and butterflies.

Common name White clover
Height/spread 10cm x 50cm (4in x 20in) **Foliage** Evergreen
Exposure Full sun to partial shade
Hardiness H7

Prunella vulgaris

Small and low-growing, this plant has rooting stems that allow the foliage to stay green through summer. It thrives in shade or sun and provides food for pollinators during summer, if the short spikes of violet flowers are not removed by close mowing.

Common name Selfheal
Height/spread 10cm x 50cm (4in x 20in) **Foliage** Semi-evergreen
Exposure Full sun to partial shade
Hardiness H5

Lotus corniculatus

This low-growing, spreading perennial legume thrives in poor soils, staying green by fixing its own nitrogen from the air. It bears yellow, pea-like flowers from late spring to autumn, which are attractive to pollinators.

Common name Bird's foot trefoil
Height/spread 20cm x 50cm (8in x 20in)
Foliage Semi-evergreen **Exposure** Full sun **Hardiness** H7

Bellis perennis

A low-growing, spreading perennial that thrives in short turf and poor soils. It stays green in dry conditions and tolerates mowing, making it ideal for species-rich lawns. White flowers with yellow centres bloom from early spring through to early autumn, providing a long-lasting nectar source for pollinators.

Common name Daisy **Height/spread** to 10cm x 10cm (4in x 4in) **Foliage** Evergreen **Exposure** Full sun to partial shade **Hardiness** H7

GROUND COVER TO REPLACE LAWNS

Thymus serpyllum

This ground-hugging, drought-tolerant herb forms a dense mat of small, aromatic leaves, perfect for minimizing water loss and creating ground cover. It thrives in poor, well-drained soils and produces small, purple flowers in late spring and early summer that attract pollinators.

Common name Wild thyme, creeping thyme
Height/spread 10cm x 30cm (4in x 12in)
Foliage Evergreen **Exposure** Full sun
Hardiness H5

Sedum acre

A resilient, mat-forming succulent that can thrive in poor, dry soils because its tiny fleshy leaves are able to retain moisture. It makes perfect ground cover for sunny, dry areas and tolerates light foot traffic. The small, yellow, star-shaped flowers bloom in summer.

Common name Biting stonecrop
Height/spread 10cm x 40cm (4in x 16in)
Foliage Evergreen **Exposure** Full sun
Hardiness H7

Dymondia margaretae

A perennial that forms a dense, low-growing mat of narrow, silvery foliage that reflects heat and minimizes water loss, making this ideal drought-tolerant ground cover for full sun, in gardens where winters are mild. Creates a soft, carpet-like appearance with small yellow flowers in summer.

Common name Silver carpet
Height/spread 10cm x 30cm (4in x 12in)
Foliage Evergreen **Exposure** Full sun
Hardiness H3

Phyla nodiflora (syn. *Lippia nodiflora*)

Capeweed's tough, waxy, low-growing foliage conserves moisture and creates dense ground cover that forms a resilient and low-care lawn alternative. A profusion of fragrant white or pink flowerheads appears on upright stems in summer, attracting pollinating insects.

Common name Capeweed
Height/spread 10cm x 50cm (4in x 20in)
Foliage Semi-evergreen   **Exposure** Full sun to part shade   **Hardiness** H4

Mentha requienii

This hardy, low-growing mint forms a dense mat of slender, root-forming stems, which allow it to access moisture in poor soils. Its rounded, aromatic, bright green leaves create lush ground cover, and plants also bear spikes of tiny purple flowers in summer, which are valuable for pollinators. A great lawn alternative for dry, shaded areas.

Common name Corsican mint
Height/spread 10cm x 60cm (4in x 24in)
Foliage Semi-evergreen
Exposure Partial shade to full shade
Hardiness H7

BIBLIOGRAPHY & RESOURCES
Chapter 1

14 "Read the RHS Sustainability Strategy", RHS, rhs.org.uk/science/sustainability/sustainability-strategy-document

14 "Climate change and water-related disasters", UN Environment Programme, unep.org/topics/fresh-water/disasters-and-climate-change/climate-change-and-water-related-disasters

14 Douville, H., K. Raghavan, J. Renwick, R.P. Allan, P.A. Arias, M. Barlow, R. Cerezo-Mota, A. Cherchi, T.Y. Gan, J. Gergis, D. Jiang, A. Khan, W. Pokam Mba, D. Rosenfeld, J. Tierney, and O. Zolina, 2021: Water Cycle Changes. In *Climate Change 2021: The Physical Science Basis. Contribution of Working Group I to the Sixth Assessment Report of the Intergovernmental Panel on Climate Change.* Cambridge University Press, pp.1055–1210,
doi: 10.1017/9781009157896.010

14 "Human rights to water and sanitation", United Nations, unwater.org/water-facts/human-rights-water-and-sanitation

16 "Global water crisis: facts, FAQs, and how to help", World Vision, 9 August 2024, worldvision.org/clean-water-news-stories/global-water-crisis-facts

16 "25 countries, housing one quarter of the population, face extremely high water stress." Samantha Kuzma, Liz Saccoccia, Marlena Chertock, 16 August 2023, World Resources Institute, wri.org/insights/highest-water-stressed-countries

18 "How is climate change impacting the water cycle?", Carly Dodd, 15 September 2021, WorldAtlas, worldatlas.com/articles/how-is-climate-change-impacting-the-water-cycle.html

18 "Condensation", National Geographic, education.nationalgeographic.org/resource/condensation/

18 William H. Schlesinger, Scott Jasechko, "Transpiration in the global water cycle", *Agricultural and forest meteorology*, vol.189–190, 1 June 2014, pp.115–117. doi.org/10.1016/j.agrformet.2014.01.011

22 "Extreme weather", World Meteorological Organization, wmo.int/topics/extreme-weather

22 "How much has the Earth's temperature changed in the last 100 years? And what does that mean for us?", Professor Zanna Chase, Curious Climate, University of Tasmania, curiousclimate.org.au/ccs_questions/how-much-has-the-earths-temperature-changed-in-the-last-100-years-and-what-does-that-mean-for-us/

22 "How is climate linked to extreme weather?", Met Office, metoffice.gov.uk/weather/climate/climate-and-extreme-weather

22 "Attributing extreme weather to climate change.", Met Office, metoffice.gov.uk/research/climate/understanding-climate/attributing-extreme-weather-to-climate-change

24 "Where does your water come from – and how can you keep it clean?", Lisa Beach, 3 August 2020, NEEF, neefusa.org/story/water/where-does-your-water-come-and-how-can-you-keep-it-clean

24 "What are blue, green, and grey water?", American Society of Agronomy (ASA), Crop Science Society of America (CSSA), Soil Science Society of America (SSSA), 17 January 2022, Newswise, newswise.com/articles/what-are-blue-green-and-grey-water

26 "Water scarcity", Melissa Petruzzello, 11 January 2025, Britannica, britannica.com/topic/water-scarcity

26 "Water Scarcity", Food and Agriculture Organisation of the United Nations, fao.org/land-water/water/water-scarcity/en/

27 "Leakage in the water industry", 21 November 2022, Ofwat, ofwat.gov.uk/leakage-in-the-water-industry/

27 "The United Nations World Water Development Report 2024: water for prosperity and peace", UNESCO World Water Assessment Programme, 2024, unesdoc.unesco.org/ark:/48223/pf0000388948

28 "Summer 2024 was world's hottest on record", Simon King, 6 September 2024, BBC Weather, www.bbc.co.uk/weather/articles/c93p5kz9elro

28 "The London climate resilience review", July 2024, Emma Howard Boyd CBE, George Leigh, Johanna Sutton, www.london.gov.uk/sites/default/files/2024-07/The_London_Climate_Resilience_Review_July_2024_FA.pdf

28 "The 11 cities most likely to run out of drinking water – like Cape Town", 11 February 2018, BBC News, bbc.co.uk/news/world-42982959

30 "How much water do you use?", CCW, www.ccw.org.uk/save-money-and-water/averagewateruse/

33 "'Mains to Rains' pledge: Water the way nature intended", RHS and Cranfield University, mains2rains.uk

34 "Combined sewer overflows explained", 2 July 2020, Paige Chaplin, Environment Agency, environmentagency.blog.gov.uk/2020/07/02/combined-sewer-overflows-explained/

36 "Water harvesting", 2025, Brad Lancaster, Rainwater harvesting for drylands and beyond, www.harvestingrainwater.com/water-harvesting/

37 "Hardness of water", 11 June 2018, Water Science School USGS, www.usgs.gov/special-topics/water-science-school/science/hardness-water

39 WaterAid, wateraid.org

Chapter 2

54 "What size rainwater tank do I need?", Owls Hall, www.owlshall.co.uk/guide/rainwater-harvesting/what-size-rainwater-tank-do-i-need

54 "Rainwater harvesting calculator", December 29 2017, Rain Harvest, www.rainharvest.co.za/2017/12/rainwater-harvesting-calculator-south-africa/

58 "Condensate and dew harvesting", "Fog harvesting", "Snow and wind harvesting", 2025, Brad Lancaster, Rainwater harvesting for drylands and beyond, www.harvestingrainwater.com/

61 "Watering", RHS, rhs.org.uk/garden-jobs/watering

66 Hamlyn G. Jones,"Can water droplets on leaves cause leaf scorch?", *New Phytologist*, 2010, Vol 185, 4, pages 865–867, doi.org/10.1111/j.1469-8137.2009.03161.x

68 Irrigatia solar automatic watering system, irrigatia.com

70 "Using grey water", RHS, www.rhs.org.uk/science/gardening-in-a-changing-world/water-use-in-gardens/using-grey-water

Chapter 3

74 "Passive and active rainwater harvesting – what's the difference?", 2017, Permasystems, permasystems.org/blog/passive-and-active-rainwater-harvesting

76 "Managed aquifer recharge", Katja Luxem, Sept 2017, American Geosciences Institute, www.americangeosciences.org/static/files/profession/geoscience-currents/CI_Factsheet_2017_6_MAR_170921.pdf

77 "What are sustainable drainage systems (SuDS)?", Mary Richards, 25 March 2024, Grand Designs Magazine, granddesignsmagazine.com/garden/landscaping/what-are-sustainable-drainage-systems-suds/

79 "Pictorial meadows and the greening of Sheffield: a Grey to Green SuDS success story", Pictorial Meadows, Sept 6 2024, pictorialmeadows.co.uk/blogs/blog/pictorial-meadows-and-the-greening-of-sheffield-a-grey-to-green-suds-success-story

82 "Rain gardens", RHS, rhs.org.uk/garden-features/rain-gardens

89 "Biosolar green roofs – combining solar panels and green roofs", Livingroofs.org, livingroofs.org/introduction-types-green-roof/biosolar-green-roofs-solar-green-roofs/

89 "Green roofs", US General Services Administration, gsa.gov/governmentwide-initiatives/federal-highperformance-buildings/resource-library/integrative-strategies/green-roofs

Chapter 4

93 "Soil and water relationships", Jeff Ball, Noble Research Institute, noble.org/regenerative-agriculture/soil/soil-and-water-relationships/

94 "Landscape mulch for water conservation", Kelly Feehan, April 30 2024, University of Nebraska-Lincoln Institute of Agriculture and Natural Resources, water.unl.edu/article/lawns-gardens-landscapes/landscape-mulch-water-conservation/

96 Kevin Handreck, *Good Gardens with Less Water* (CSIRO Publishing Gardening Guides Series, 2008)

100 "Life under your feet – feeding plants and the planet", Marc Redmile-Gordon, 5 Dec 2023, RHS, rhs.org.uk/science/articles/life-under-your-feet

102 Charles Dowding, *No dig: Nurture your soil to grow better veg with less effort* (DK, 2022)

102 "The magic of soil – and de-mystifying no-dig", Sheila Das, 4 Dec 2023, RHS, rhs.org.uk/gardening-for-the-environment/the-magic-of-soil

Chapter 6

140 "The physiology of adventitious roots", Bianca Steffens, Amanda Rasmussen, *Plant Physiology*, 2015 Dec 23;170(2):603–617, doi: 10.1104/pp.15.01360

143 "Plant adaptations of wetland plants", Cindy Hagley, University of Minnesota, www.d.umn.edu/~vbrady/WE_website/wetlands101/WE-lectures/Plant%20Adaptation.pdf

FURTHER READING

BOOKS

Bradbury, Kate *RHS How to Create a Wildlife Pond: Plan, Dig, and Enjoy a Natural Pond in Your Own Back Garden* (DK, 2021)

Chatto, Beth *Drought-Resistant Planting: Lessons from Beth Chatto's Gravel Garden* (Francis Lincoln, 2016)

Clayton, Philip *Parched: 50 plants that thrive and survive in a dry garden* (Welbeck, 2024)

Dowding, Charles *No Dig: Nurture Your Soil to Grow Better Veg with Less Effort* (DK, 2022)

Dunnett, Nigel *Naturalistic Planting Design The Essential Guide: How to Design High-Impact, Low-Input Gardens* (Filbert Press, 2019)

Dunnett, Nigel and Clayden, Andy *Rain Gardens: Managing Water Sustainably in the Garden and Designed Landscape* (Timber Press, 2007)

Filippi, Olivier *The Dry Gardening Handbook: Plants and Practices for a Changing Climate* (Filbert Press, 2019)

Handreck, Kevin *Good Gardens with Less Water* (CSIRO Publishing Gardening Guides Series, 2008)

Korn, Peter *Peter Korn's Garden: Giving Plants What They Want* (Peter Korn, 2013)

Lancaster, Brad *Rainwater Harvesting for Drylands and Beyond: Volume 1 Guiding Principles to Welcome Rain into your Life and Landscape* (Rainsource Press, 2019)

Lancaster, Brad *Rainwater Harvesting for Drylands and Beyond: Volume 2 Water-Harvesting Earthworks* (Rainsource Press, 2019)

Massey, Tom *RHS Resilient Garden: Sustainable Gardening for a Changing Climate* (DK, 2023)

Nex, Sally *RHS How to Garden the Low-Carbon Way: The Steps You Can Take to Help Combat Climate Change* (DK, 2021)

Philip Williams, Kevin and Guidi, Michael *Shrouded in Light: Naturalistic Planting Inspired by Wild Shrublands* (Filbert Press, 2024)

Rainer, Thomas *Planting in a Post-Wild World: Designing Plant Communities for Resilient Landscapes* (Timber Press, 2015)

RESEARCH PAPERS AND REPORTS

"The United Nations World Water Development Report 2024: water for prosperity and peace", 2024.
unesdoc.unesco.org/ark:/48223/pf0000388948

This report emphasizes the vital global role of sustainable water management.

"Water Cycle Changes. In Climate Change 2021: The Physical Science Basis. Contribution of Working Group I to the Sixth Assessment Report of the Intergovernmental Panel on Climate Change", 2021, Douville, H., K. Raghavan, J. Renwick, R.P. Allan, P.A. Arias, M. Barlow, R. Cerezo-Mota, A. Cherchi, T.Y. Gan, J. Gergis, D. Jiang, A. Khan, W. Pokam Mba, D. Rosenfeld, J. Tierney, and O. Zolina, Cambridge University Press, pp.1055–1210, doi:10.1017/9781009157896.010

Information highlighting ways that global warming intensifies the water cycle, leading to more extreme precipitation, prolonged droughts, and shifts in regional water availability.

"Realising Global Water Futures: a Summary of Progress in Delivering Solutions to Water Threats in an Era of Global Change.", 2024, Global Water Futures.
gwf.usask.ca

A Canadian research initiative focused on improving disaster warning systems, predicting water quantity and quality, and developing risk management tools.

"Four billion people lack safe water", Rob Hope, Science, 385, 708–709 (2024)
doi:10.1126/science.adr3271

A study drawing attention to the fact that over 4.4 billion people lack access to safe household drinking water, underscoring the critical need for sustainable water management practices.

"RHS Gardening in a Changing Climate", 2017, Eleanor Webster, Ross Cameron, and Alastair Culham, Royal Horticultural Society, UK.
rhs.org.uk/science/gardening-in-a-changing-world/climate-change

This report provides guidance on how climate change affects gardening practices, highlighting both challenges and opportunities for gardeners.

WEBSITES

Charles Dowding – No Dig Gardening
charlesdowding.co.uk
No dig gardening can protect and improve soil structure, increasing moisture retention. Charles Dowding is a leading expert.

Ecosure
ecosure.co.uk
Supplier of water butts and plastic and steel water tanks.

Garden Organic – Soil management
gardenorganic.org.uk/expert-advice/garden-management/soil
Offers insights into organic soil management techniques that support water conservation.

Global Commission on the Economics of Water
watercommission.org/
This organization examines the economic value of water, advocating for policies that encourage water conservation and sustainable water use.

Mains to Rains
mains2rains.uk
Encourages gardeners to reduce reliance on mains water by harvesting and using rainwater efficiently, helping to mitigate water scarcity.

Pictorial Meadows
pictorialmeadows.co.uk
Meadows are a sustainable and drought-resilient choice for planting. Meadow seed and turf products available here as well as general advice.

Rainwater Terrace
rainwater-terrace.com
Manufacturer and distributor of modular water butts with built-in planters.

RHS Advice
A comprehensive and wide-ranging online resource covering various horticultural topics, including water-efficient gardening practices.
rhs.org.uk

Composting
rhs.org.uk/soil-composts-mulches/composting
Compost improves soil structure and water retention, reducing the need for watering.

Drought-Resistant Plants
rhs.org.uk/plants/for-places/drought-resistant
A curated list of resilient plants that thrive with minimal water, for low-maintenance landscapes.

Grey Water
rhs.org.uk/science/gardening-in-a-changing-world/water-use-in-gardens/using-grey-water
Guidance on the safe use of household grey water to reduce dependence on mains water for irrigation.

Mulches and Mulching
www.rhs.org.uk/soil-composts-mulches/mulch
Mulching reduces evaporation, suppresses weeds, and improves soil moisture retention.

No Dig Gardening
rhs.org.uk/soil-composts-mulches/no-dig-gardening
Preserving soil structure through no dig gardening enhances its ability to retain water.

Rain Gardens
rhs.org.uk/garden-features/rain-gardens
Explains how rain gardens help manage stormwater, reduce flooding, and maximize rainwater absorption into the landscape.

RHS Grow App
rhs.org.uk/rhsgrow
A digital tool to help gardeners make informed decisions about plant care, including water-efficient gardening and plant identification.

RHS Strategy to 2030
rhs.org.uk/about-us/what-we-do/rhs-strategy-to-2030
Sets out how the RHS plans to be net positive for nature and people by 2030.

RHS Sustainability Strategy
rhs.org.uk/science/sustainability
Outlines RHS strategies for sustainable gardening, including water conservation practices that can be applied at all scales.

Wildlife ponds
rhs.org.uk/ponds/wildlife-ponds
Ponds are a sustainable way to store water, support biodiversity, and can help nearby plants thrive with less irrigation.

Susdrain – Sustainable Drainage Systems (SuDS)
susdrain.org
A key resource on sustainable drainage, with solutions to reduce rainwater runoff and water waste in urban and garden settings.

UN Water
unwater.org/
Global insights into water management, including strategies for sustainable water use in agriculture and landscaping.

Water Butts Direct
waterbuttsdirect.co.uk
Supplier of a wide range of water butts, including decorative and underground options.

Water Harvesting
harvestingrainwater.com/water-harvesting
A resource with practical techniques for capturing and utilizing rainwater, which can reduce reliance on mains water for irrigation.

Page numbers in **bold** refer to main entries

A

Acer campestre 169
Achillea millefolium 145, 179
   A. 'Moonshine' 149
adaptability, building in 108
adventitious roots 143
aerenchyma 143
African lily 'Midnight Star' 149
Agapanthus 'Midnight Star' 149
aggregates 96
agriculture 16, 20, 27
Ahn, Je 40–43
AI harvesting systems **65**
air conditioning units 58
air source heat pumps 58
air wells 58
Ajuga reptans 167
alder, common 169
algal growth 53
Alisma plantago-aquatica 171
alluvial landscapes 136
Alnus glutinosa 169
Alyssum montanum 158
Anemanthele lessoniana 152
aquifers 24, 76, 77
Arbutus andrachne 155
Arctic 22
arid regions 26
Armeria maritima 158
Aronia melanocarpa 166
arrowhead 177
arum lily 177
Astilbe rivularis 170
   A. × *arendsii* 170
Athyrium filix-femina 168
attenuation 35
   attenuation tanks 89
automated drip irrigation systems **64**

B

bark 32, 96
Barton, Kevin 79
basins 57
basket of gold 158
bath water 70
beeblossom 151
bee's primrose 174
berms 74, **84**, 126
Betula nigra 169
biodiversity 74, 75, 79, 80, 86, 136
biosolar roofs **89**, 119
bird's foot trefoil 179
bistort, common 176
Bistorta affinis (syn. *Persicaria affinis*) 167
   B. *officinalis* (syn. *P. bistorta*) 176
biting stonecrop 180
black birch 169
black chokeberry 166
black iris 162
black water 24–25, 36
blue-green roofs 89
blue roofs **89**

blue water 24–25
bog gardens 108
bogbean 174
Bowles's golden sedge 171
broussa mullein 149
brown-eyed Susan 160
bugle 167
Bulbine frutescens 159
Butomus umbellatus 171

C

Calamagrostis brachytricha 164
calcium 39
Calla palustris 171
Caltha palustris 171
Camassia leichtlinii 163
candytuft, perennial 157
capeweed 181
carbon 94
   carbon sinks 101
cardinal flower 173
Carex elata 'Aurea' 171
   C. *morrowii* 'Irish Green' 164
   C. *remota* 163
   C. *testacea* 152
Castlefield Viaduct 42
catchment areas 108
catmint 150
Centranthus lecoqii 150
   C. *ruber* 150
Ceratostigma plumbaginoides 151
Cercis canadensis 169
Chinese rhubarb 161
cinnamon fern 174
Cistus × *purpureus* 155
clay soil 60, 62, **92**, 93
climate change 14, 16, 37
   and extreme weather **22–23**, 77
   impact on rainfall 20, 22, 37
   lawns 145
   and the water cycle **20–21**
   and water scarcity 26
clouds 18, 19
clover 102, 145, 179
coagulation 25
coastal flooding 20
compost 32, 60
   compost mulch 96, 97
   composting at home **102**
composting bins 102, 119
condensation **18**, 19, 20
   condensate harvesting 38, **58**
containers and pots 117
   watering 60, 61, 62
contamination 47, 53, 69, 70, 71
Cornus sanguinea 165
Corsican mint 181
Cranfield University 33–35, 71
creeping Jenny 167
creeping thyme 145, 157, 180
crevice gardens: how to build **123**
   plants for **156–59**
Crocosmia 'Lucifer' 161
Cyperus giganteus 172

D

damp depressions, plants for **160–69**

Das, Sheila **98–99**
Deschampsia cespitosa 163
detergents 70, 71
developing world, effect of water crisis on 14, 17
dew harvesting 38, **58**
dew point **58**
Dianthus deltoides 157
dig vs no dig gardening 99
dish washing 70
dogwood, common 165
dotted loosestrife 163
downpipes 46, 74, 113
   disconnecting 32, **36–37**, 47, 115
   rainwater diverter kits 48
Draba aizoides 158
drainage 22, 89
   soakaways 57, 84, **87**
   Sustainable Drainage Systems (SuDS) 77, 80, 81
drip irrigation systems, automated **64–65**
driveways 28, 37, 88, 110
drought 16, 20, 22
   lawns and 145
   plant adaptations to **142**, 148
dry areas, plants for **148–55**
Dryopteris filix-mas 168
Dunnett, Professor Nigel 78
dwarf bulrush 170
Dymondia margaretae 180

E

earthworks 108
   using to manage water **84–87**
eastern redbud 169
Echinops ritro 149
Edible Bristol (EB) 34–35
El Niño 22
Elaeagnus 'Quicksilver' 154
elder, common 166
energy demands 16
ephemeral ponds 74, 84, **86**, 111, 118
   building **130–31**
   natural 136
   plants for **160–69**
Equisetum hyemale 172
Eriogonum umbellatum 158
eulalia 164
Eupatorium maculatum Atropurpureum Group 161
evaporation **18**, 19, 20, 32, 66, 94
evapotranspiration **18**, 24
Extracellular Polymeric Substances 101

F

feather grass 153
ferns **168**
Festuca amethystina 152
field maple 169
Filipendula rubra 'Venusta' 172
   F. *ulmaria* 162
filtration 25, 53
   grey water 70, 71
   irrigation systems 68
   rain gardens 82

rainwater harvesting 47, 53
fires 22
floc 25
flocculation 25
flooding 16, 28, 32, 36, 37, 88
   flash floods 20, 77
   impact of climate change on 22
   managing tank overflow 57
   plant adaptations to **143**
   reducing risk of 74, 81, 82
   types of **20**
   urban flooding 20, 77
flowering rush 171
fluoride 25
fog harvesting 38, **59**
foliage, drought adaptations 142
fungal hyphae 99, 100, 101, 105

G

garden waste 96
germander sage 148
Geum rivale 175
Giardia 53
Giving Back 42
global warming 20, 22, 28
global water crisis **14–17**
globe thistle 149
grasses 136
   choosing the right lawn grass 145
   for dry areas **152–53**
   for rain gardens and temporarily wet areas **163–64**
grasslands 136
gravel 32, 33, 77, 88, 94, 96
gravity-fed systems 108
great burnet 162
Grecian strawberry tree 155
green manures 102
green roofs 53, 77, **89**, 114
green water 24, 36
greenhouse gases 22
grey club-rush 175
Grey to Green **78–81**
grey water 24–25, 36, 38
   understanding and using **70–71**
Griffiths, Professor Alistair 66
ground cover: plants to replace lawns **180–81**
   for rain gardens and temporarily wet areas **167**
groundwater 24, 28, 30, 33, 74
   recharging 76, 77, 84
guelder rose 165
Gush, Dr Mark 66, **68–69**
guttering 36, 46, 47, 48

H

hail 18, 19
hard landscaping 28, 33, 108, 110, 111
   see also paving, *etc*
hardy blue-flowered leadwort 151
heart-leaved houttuynia 173
heat: heatwaves 22, 28
   plant adaptations to 142
Helleborus argutifolius 150

Hemerocallis lilioasphodelus 161
hens and chicks 157
holly-leaved hellebore 150
hosepipes 28, 62
houseleek, common 157
Houttuynia cordata 173
humans: human factor 22
   human rights to water and sanitation 14
Hydrangea quercifolia 166
hydroponic growing system 119, **129**
hydrozoning 33, **135**
Hylotelephium spectabile 151

I

Iberis sempervirens 157
ice plant 151
impermeable surfaces: problems caused by 77, 108, 110, 112, 113
   soakaways **87**
infiltration 18, 19, 103
   earthworks and 84, 85, 108
   passive rainwater harvesting 74
   permeable surfaces 77, 88
infrastructure 16, 26
inspiration, sources of **136–37**
interception 18
Iris chrysographes 162
   I. laevigata 173
   I. sibirica 161
irrigation *see individual methods*

J

Japanese rose 166
Joe-Pye weed 161
Johannesburg 26
Juncus effusus 173

K

Korean feather reed grass 164
Korn, Peter **104–105**

L

lady fern 168
lakes 24
Lavandula × intermedia 'Grosso' 155
lavender 'Grosso' 155
lawns 77
   additions to grass lawns **179**
   ground cover to replace lawns **180–81**
   planting waterwise lawns **144–45**
   plants for waterwise lawns **178–81**
   watering 33, 61
leaking pipes 27
leaves: adaptations to wet conditions and flooding 143
   drought adaptations 142
   leaf scorch **66**
   water loss from 67
lesser knotweed 167
lesser spearwort 176
Lewisia cotyledon 159
lifelong saxifrage 156

loamy soils **92**, 93
Lobelia cardinalis 173
location, watering and 60
Lotus corniculatus 179
Lysimachia nummularia 167
   L. punctata 163
Lythrum salicaria 162

M

maiden pink 157
Mains to Rains 33, **34–35**
male fern 168
Manning, Janet 34–35
marsh fern 175
marsh marigold 171
Matteuccia struthiopteris 168
mauve valerian 150
meadow buttercup 177
meadows 136
meadowsweet 162, 172
membranes, weed suppressant 94
Mentha requienii 181
Menyanthes trifoliata 174
metal walkway gratings 120
Mexican papyrus 172
Mexico City 26
microbes 99, 101, 102
mineral mulches 96, 126
Miscanthus sinensis 164
Molinia caerulea 164
montbretia 'Lucifer' 161
morrow's sedge 'Irish Green' 164
mosquitoes 53
mulches and mulching **94–95**, 102
   mulch application 32, **97**, 126
   planting in pure sand **104–105**
   selecting the right mulch **96–97**
mycorrhizal fungi 99, 100, 101, 105, 139
Myosotis scorpioides 175

N

native species 135, 136
natural landscapes, taking inspiration from **136–37**
Nepeta × faassenii 150
New Zealand blue grass 152
Nicolson, Harold 139
no-dig gardening 99, **102–103**
non-revenue water 26–27

O

oak-leaved hydrangea 166
Oenothera lindheimeri 151
oleaster 'Quicksilver' 154
orange New Zealand sedge 152
oregano 150
organic matter **92**, 101
   organic mulches 94, **96–97**, 99, 102
Origanum vulgare 150
osmosis 101
Osmunda cinnamomea 174
ostrich fern 168
overflow, planning for 108

P

pasque flower 157

passive irrigation systems **53**, 57, 62
passive rainwater harvesting 57, **72–89**, 114
  collecting and managing rainwater naturally **74–75**
  green, blue, and biosolar roofs **89**
  permeable surfaces **76–77**, 88
  rain gardens **82–83**
  using earthworks to manage water **84–87**
patios 28, 123
paving: laid on a mortar bed and/or concrete base 122
  laid on a sand bed 122
  permeable 33, 57, 77, **88**, 108, 115, 118, **120–22**
  problems caused by 33, 77, 110, 117
peace, water and the threat to world 27
perennials: for dry areas **148–51**
  for rain gardens and temporarily wet areas **160–63**
permafrost 22
permanent wilting point 93
permeable surfaces 118, **120–22**
  importance of **76–77**
  permeable paving 33, 57, 77, **88**, 108, 115, 118, **120–22**
pheasant's tail 152
Phlomis fruticosa 154
  P. purpurea 154
Phyla nodiflora (syn. *Lippia nodiflora*) 181
plants **132–81**
  adaptations to drought or extreme heat **142**, 148
  adaptations to wet conditions and flooding **143**
  available water for **93**
  choosing 28, 30, 33, **134–35**
  for crevice gardens **156–59**
  effective watering techniques **62–65**
  hydrozoning 33, **135**
  and improving soil permeability **103**
  leaf scorch **66**
  mulching 94
  plant directory **146–81**
  plants for dry areas **148–55**
  post-planting care 140
  preference for rainwater 39
  for rain gardens and temporarily wet areas **160–69**
  for reliably wet areas **170–77**
  resilient plants for swales 79
  watering **60–61, 66–67**
  for waterwise lawns **178–81**
  waterwise plant adaptations **140–43**
Poa labillardierei 152
polar regions 22
pollutants 53, 81, 82
pollution 26, 36, 37, 77
pomegranate 155

ponding depth 126
ponds *see* ephemeral ponds
pores 92
pots and containers 33, 117
  watering 60, 61, 62
Primula beesiana 174
  P. vialii 176
prostrate speedwell 159
Prunella vulgaris 179
Pulsatilla vulgaris 157
Punica granatum 155
purple-flowered rock rose 155
purple Jerusalem sage 154
purple loosestrife 162
purple moor grass 164
purple willow 165

R
rain gardens 77, **82–83**, 111, 114
  creating a rain garden **124–27**
  earthworks and 84
  ephemeral ponds 86, 136
  plants for **160–69**
rainfall 18, 19, 94
  heavy rainfall 36, 74
  impact of climate change on 16, 20, 22, 37
  variability in **57**
rainwater diverter kits **48**
rainwater harvesting **36–71**, 119
  active harvesting 28, 30, 32, 38, **44–71**, 74
  collecting and managing rainwater naturally **74–75**
  dangers of storing rainwater 53
  disconnecting downpipes 32, **36–37**
  filtration 47, 53
  importance of permeable surfaces **76–77**
  passive rainwater harvesting 38, 39, 57, **72–89**, 114
  rain gardens **82–83**
  rooftop rainwater harvesting **46–49, 54–57**, 119
  smart rainwater harvesting systems **65**
  storing rooftop-harvested rainwater **48–51**
rainwater harvesting tanks 32, 62, 119
  above and below ground **50–51**
  automated drip irrigation systems **64**
  calculating capacity **54–55**
  calculating water usage **56**
  filtration 47
  managing overflow **57**
  supplying passive irrigation systems **53**
  uses for stored rainwater **56**
  variability in rainfall **57**
Ranunculus acris 177
  R. flammula 176
recharge trenches 84, **87**
red valerian 150
Redmile-Gordon, Dr Marc 100
remote sedge 163

reservoirs 24
Rheum palmatum 161
RHS (Royal Horticultural Society) 33–35
  RHS Chelsea Flower Show 14, 38, **40–43**, 86
  RHS Planet-Friendly Gardening Campaign **98–99**
rivers 20, 24
roadside verges 136
Robert Bray Associates 79
roofs: green, blue and biosolar roofs 77, **89**, 114, 119
  rooftop rainwater harvesting **46–49, 54–57**, 119
roots: adaptations to conditions 142, 143
  drip irrigation at the roots 69
  and mycorrhizal fungi 99, 100, 101, 105, 139
  types of 140, 141
  water uptake 67, 103, 140
Rosa rugosa 166
rough horsetail 172
Rudbeckia triloba 'Prairie Glow' 160
runoff 18, 81
  impermeable surfaces 37, 38, 77, 113
  reducing 32, 33, 74, 88, 94, 95
rush, common 173
Russian sage 151

S
Sackville-West, Vita 139
Sagittaria sagittifolia 177
Salix alba 169
  S. purpurea 165
Salvia 'Blue Spire' (syn. *Perovskia* 'Blue Spire') 151
  S. chamaedryoides 148
Sambucus nigra 166
sand 96
  paving laid on a sand bed 122
  planting in pure sand **104–105**
  sandy soil 60, 62, **92**, 93
Sanguisorba officinalis 162
sanitation 14, 17
saturation point 93
Saxifraga paniculata 156
Schoenoplectus lacustris subsp. *tabernaemontani* 175
scorched leaves **66**
sea pink 158
seasons: seasonal changes 26, 28
  watering requirements 60
sedimentation 25
Sedum 89, 151
  S. acre 180
self heal 179
semi-arid regions 26
Sempervivum tectorum 157
sewer systems 16, 24–25
  sewage discharge 28, 36–37, 77
shade 135
Sheffield Grey to Green **78–81**
shower water 70
shrubs: for dry areas **154–55**

for rain gardens and temporarily wet areas **165–66**
shuttlecock fern 168
Siberian iris 161
Siberian waldsteinia 167
silver carpet 180
Siskiyou Lewisia 159
Sissinghurst Castle Garden **138–39**
smart rainwater harvesting systems 65
Smith, Troy Scott **138–39**
smooth iris 173
snow 18, 19
   harvesting 38, **59**
soakaways 57, 84, **87**
society garlic 151
soft rush 173
soil: attenuation 35
   clay soils 60, 62, **92**, 93
   composition of 60
   exposed 116
   improving permeability with plants 103
   loamy soils **92**, 93
   no-dig gardening 99, **102–103**
   nurturing **90–105**
   pH 97, 135
   ponding depth 126
   sandy soil 60, 62, **92**, 93, **104–105**
   soil erosion 57, 74, 77, 84, 94, 95, 103
   soil health 30, 32, 35, 74, 99, **100–101**
   soil types 66, 92, 126
   water evaporation 66, 67
   as a water store **92–93**
   waterlogging **93**
   see also mulches and mulching
solar powered irrigation system **68–69**
sprinkler systems 62
Stachys byzantine 71
stalked bulbine 159
stems 143
Stipa pseudoichu 153
storms 22
stormwater: harvesting 38, 82, 89
   stormwater runoff 32, 33, 37, 74, 77, 113
   Sustainable Drainage Systems (SuDS) 77, 81
Studio Weave **40–45**
sulphur flower 158
surface water 18, 24
Surfers Against Sewage **37**
Sustainable Drainage Systems (SuDS) 77, **78–81**
sustainable gardens, tips for **32–35**
swales 57, 74, 75, 79, 84, **85**
   plants for 79, **160–69**

T
tap water **24–25**, 28, 39
temperatures: rise in global 20, 22
   soil temperature regulation 94

Teucrium fruticans 154
Thelypteris palustris 175
thrift 158
throughflow 19
thyme 157, 180
Thymus serpyllum 145, 157, 180
timers 64
transpiration 18, 19, 60, 66, 103
tree germander 154
trees: for dry areas **155**
   for rain gardens and temporarily wet areas **169**
trenches, recharge 84, **87**
Trifolium repens 145, 179
tufted fescue 152
tufted hair grass 163
Tulbaghia violacea 151
tulip 'Eastern Star' 159
Tulipa humilis 'Eastern Star' 159
Typha minima 177

U
UK Climate Change Committee 28
United Nations 14
   UN Food and Agriculture Organisation (FAO) 26
   UN World Water Development Report 27
urban environments, plants in 136
urban flooding 20, 77

V
Venn, Sarah 35
Verbascum bombyciferum 149
Veronica prostrata 159
vetch 102
vial's primrose 176
Viburnum opulus 165

W
Waldsteinia ternata 167
walkways **120–22**
waste water 24–25, 36, 38
water: harvesting **36–89**, 114
   soil as a water store **92–93**
   where tap water comes from **24–25**
water arum 171
water avens 175
water butts 32, 38, 47, 118
   improving the appearance of **128**
   installing **48–49**
   solar powered irrigation system **68–69**
water cycle **18–21**, 30, 35
water forget-me-not 175
water plantain 171
water scarcity **26–27**, 28
water stress **16–17**, 26
water treatment 24–25, 37, 39
water usage 30
water vapour 18, 19, 24, 58
WaterAid 14, **41**
   RHS Chelsea Flower Show garden 38, **40–43**, 86

waterborne diseases 53
watering: effective watering techniques **62–65**
   no-irrigation gardening **138–39**
   solar powered irrigation system **68–69**
   sustainable **60–61**
   when to water 61, **66–67**, 140
watering cans 33, 62
waterlogging **93**, 94, 140
waterside astilbe 170
the Waterwise garden **106–31**
   crevice gardens 123
   design **108–19**
   ephemeral ponds **130–31**
   front garden 110, **112–15**, 147
   hydroponic growing system **129**
   improving the appearance of water butts **128**
   permeable walkways and paving **120–23**
   plant directory **146–81**
   rain garden **124–27**
   rear garden 111, **116–19**, 147
   side-by-side comparison **110–11**
waterwise gardening: principles of **30–31**
   tips for a sustainable garden **32–35**
weather 16, 18
   extreme weather 20, **22–23**, 77
weed suppressant membranes 94
weeds 94
wet areas, plants for reliably **170–77**
wet conditions, plant adaptations to **143**
wetlands 30, 75
white clover 179
white gaura 151
white willow 169
wild thyme 157, 180
wildfires 16, 22
wildflowers 136
wildlife 57, 75, 82, 86, 111
wood chippings 94, 96, 102

X
xeriscaping **134**

Y
yarrow 145, 179
   'Moonshine' 149
yellow daylily 161
yellow whitlow grass 158

Z
Zantedeschia aethiopica 177

ACKNOWLEDGEMENTS

PICTURE CREDITS

The publisher would like to thank the following for their kind permission to reproduce their photographs:

(Key: a-above; b-below/bottom; c-centre; f-far; l-left; r-right; t-top)

5 Alister Thorpe. **8** Britt Willoughby. **9** Wax London. **11** Alister Thorpe. **15 Dreamstime.com:** Dimamutodah (t). **GAP Photos:** Jonathan Buckley - Garden: Perch Hill (b). **20 Dreamstime.com:** Razvan25. **20–21 Alamy Stock Photo:** Jeff Morgan 04. **23 Getty Images:** David Ramos (b). **Shutterstock.com:** Brunohitam (t). **29 Alamy Stock Photo:** Stephen Connell (bl); Radharc Images (br). **GAP Photos:** Jonathan Buckley - Garden: Perch Hill (tl, tr). **31 GAP Photos:** Juliette Wade (b). **Alister Thorpe:** (t). **32 Robert Bray Associates:** Maple Photography. **33** Alister Thorpe. **34 Edible Bristol:** Noah Venn. **38 GAP Photos:** Nicola Stocken. **39 Alamy Stock Photo:** Saxon Holt. **40** Alister Thorpe. **41** Alister Thorpe: (t, b). **42–43 Studio Weave:** Je Ahn. **49 Alamy Stock Photo:** Mark Boulton (bl). **Shutterstock.com:** J.J. Gouin (tr); D J Taylor (br). **Alister Thorpe:** (tl). **50 Dreamstime.com:** Hamik. **51 GAP Photos:** Michael King. **52 Bruntwood's Bloc images courtesy of Polypipe Civils & Green Urbanisation. 57** Alister Thorpe. **59 Alamy Stock Photo:** Anton Sorokin. **63 Alamy Stock Photo:** Micheka Productions, Inh/ Michele Vitucci. **70 GAP Photos:** Victoria Frimston. **71 GAP Photos:** Victoria Frimston. **75 Alamy Stock Photo:** A.D. Fletcher (t); Saxon Holt (bl); Jonathan Ward (br). **76 Alamy Stock Photo:** Zoonar GmbH (t). **Alister Thorpe:** (b). **78** Richard Bloom. **79** Robert Bray Associates. **83 Robert Bray Associates:** Maple Photography (t). **GAP Photos:** Lilianna Sokolowska (b). **84 Alamy Stock Photo:** Saxon Holt. **85** Alister Thorpe. **86** Alister Thorpe. **87 Alamy Stock Photo:** Thomas Farlow (tr); Ian Goodrick (b). **GAP Photos:** Maxine Adcock (tl). **88 Alamy Stock Photo:** Robert K. Chin. **89 Alamy Stock Photo:** René Notenbomer. **95 GAP Photos:** Jonathan Buckley (tl); Vicki Gardner (r). **Alister Thorpe:** (bl). **96** Britt Willoughby. **97 GAP Photos:** Dave Bevan. **98 RHS:** Jason Ingram. **103 GAP Photos:** (b); Joanna Kossak (t). **104** Peter Korn. **134 Alamy Stock Photo:** RM Floral (b). **Marianne Majerus Garden Images:** Marianne Majerus – Beth Chatto Gardens, Essex (t). **137 Alamy Stock Photo:** Botany Vision (tr); Perry van Munster (tl); Chris Cole (cl); Henk van den Brink (cr); Peter J. Hatcher (b). **138 National Trust Images:** Eva Nemeth. **141 Alamy Stock Photo:** annalovisa (br); Oleg Marchak (tr); imageBROKER.com (cr). **144 Alamy Stock Photo:** Laszlo Podor. **148 GAP Photos:** (r). **149 Dorling Kindersley:** Jane Miller (ca). **GAP Photos:** Jonathan Buckley (b); J S Sira (tl); Nova Photo Graphik (tr). **150 Dorling Kindersley:** Mark Winwood / Hampton Court Flower Show 2014 (cr). **GAP Photos:** Richard Bloom (c); Elke Borkowski (t); Jo Whitworth (cl). **151 GAP Photos:** Mark Bolton (br); Frederic Didillon (tl); Neil Holmes (ca); Mark Turner (tr); J S Sira (bl). **152 GAP Photos:** Richard Bloom (tr); Jonathan Buckley (tl); Diana Jazwinski (ca); Bjorn Hansson (b). **153 Beth Chatto's Plants and Gardens. 154 Alamy Stock Photo:** Mauritius Images GmbH (tl). **GAP Photos:** Nova Photo Graphik (bl). **154–155 GAP Photos:** Jonathan Buckley. **155 Alamy Stock Photo:** Olena Kornieriera (br). **GAP Photos:** Dave Bevan (tl); Matteo Carassale (tr); Andrea Jones (bl). **156 GAP Photos:** Nova Photo Graphik (b). **157 GAP Photos:** Bjorn Hansson (ca); Nicola Stocken (tl); Nova Photo Graphik (tr); Martin Staffler (bl); Nova Photo Graphik (br). **158 GAP Photos:** Nova Photo Graphik (tl, tr, br); Rob Whitworth (bl). **159 Dorling Kindersley:** Mark Winwood / RHS Wisley (bl). **GAP Photos:** Carole Drake (br); Fiona Lea (tl); Gillian Plummer (tr). **160 GAP Photos:** John Glover (r). **161 Alamy Stock Photo:** Veronika 2V (bl). **Dorling Kindersley:** Howard Rice (br); James Young (tr). **GAP Photos:** Jonathan Buckley - Design: Keith Wiley, Wildside, Devon (tl); Robert Mabic (ca). **162 Alamy Stock Photo:** RM Floral (ca). **GAP Photos:** Mark Bolton (tr); Jonathan Buckley (tl); Elke Borkowski (b). **163 Alamy Stock Photo:** Paolo Reda - REDA & CO (tr). **GAP Photos:** Clive Nichols (tl); Visions (bl); Nova Photo Graphik (br). **164 Dorling Kindersley:** Mark Winwood / RHS Wisley (bc). **GAP Photos:** Richard Bloom (br); Visions (r); Robert Mabic (bl). **165 Dorling Kindersley:** Mark Winwood (tl). **GAP Photos:** Jonathan Buckley (tr); Jan Smith (b). **166 Dorling Kindersley:** Mark Winwood (r). **GAP Photos:** Richard Bloom (b); Jacqui Dracup (tl); Jonathan Buckley (ca). **167 Alamy Stock Photo:** Steffen Hausser / Botanikfoto (br). **GAP Photos:** Thomas Alamy (bl); John Glover (tl); Fiona Lea (tr). **168 GAP Photos:** Richard Bloom (tr); Frederic Didillon (tl); Howard Rice (b). **169 GAP Photos:** Simon Colmer (tr); Tim Gainey (tl); Jenny Lilly (ca); Rachel Warne (bl); Joanna Kossak / RHS Wisley Garden (br). **170 Alamy Stock Photo:** RM Floral (b). **171 Alamy Stock Photo:** Imago (cl). **GAP Photos:** Jonathan Buckley (tl, c); J S Sira (tr); Jonathan Buckley - Design: Carol Klein (cr). **172 GAP Photos:** Paul Debois (tr); Mark Turner (tl); Nova Photo Graphik (b). **173 Alamy Stock Photo:** Joe Blossom (bl). **Dorling Kindersley:** Peter Kindersley (tl). **GAP Photos:** Heather Edwards (br); Nova Photo Graphik (tr). **174 GAP Photos:** FhF Greenmedia (tr); Ernie Janes (l); Lynn Keddie (c). **175 GAP Photos:** Lynn Keddie (tr); J S Sira (tl); Visions (ca); James Osmond (b). **176 Dorling Kindersley:** Mark Winwood / RHS Wisley (tl). **GAP Photos:** Nova Photo Graphik (r); Joanna Kossak (bl). **177 Dorling Kindersley:** Brian North (ca). **GAP Photos:** Martin Hughes-Jones (b); Tommy Tonnesberg (tl); Visions (tr). **178 Alamy Stock Photo:** David J. Green. **179 Alamy Stock Photo:** Alice Mitchell (br); Steve Taylor ARPS (bl). **Dorling Kindersley:** Neil Hepworth (tl); Peter Kindersley (tr). **GAP Photos:** Jonathan Buckley (ca). **180 Alamy Stock Photo:** AY Images (tl); Gillian Pullinger (tr). **GAP Photos:** Jerry Pavia (b). **180–181 Alamy Stock Photo:** Frank Hekker. **181 Alamy Stock Photo:** Nature Photographers Ltd (r). **192** Wax London.

Cover images: *Front*: **Getty Images / iStock:** JoeLena b; *Back*: **Eleanor Ridsdale**

The CGI images on the following pages were created by Michael Powell © Dorling Kindersley Limited: 2, 109, 110–111, 112–113, 114–115, 116–117, 118–119, 120–121, 122, 123, 124, 127, 128, 129, 131, 142, 143, 147, 148, 156, 160, 170.

AUTHOR'S ACKNOWLEDGEMENTS

Writing my first book was a journey of discovery, and this second title has deepened my understanding of waterwise gardening and water's vital role in our landscapes. Many people deserve thanks:

My wife, Anna, for her unwavering support, even as my profession often demands so much of my time. Her keen eye for detail and gift for writing have been invaluable throughout this journey. Now, as we welcome our son, Reuben, his arrival has deepened my awareness of how vital it is to cherish our resources, especially water, and the crucial role that gardens and landscapes can play in protecting our planet's future.

Thanks to the original DK team: Ruth, Max, Chris, and Katie for their trust and vision. Thanks also to Barbara, Alastair, and Jo for keeping everything on track with creative design and editorial insight.

To the project's designers and illustrators: Vicky for engaging book design; Michael for stunning CGI garden concepts; Sweta for beautiful case study artworks; and Andrew for clear infographics. Special thanks to photographers Britt and Alister who have always captured my works so beautifully, and to picture researcher Emily for her dedication to finding perfect images to accompany the text.

I'm grateful to all interviewees: Janet Manning, Sheila Das, Peter Korn, and Troy Scott Smith, for sharing their expertise and diverse perspectives, which enrich this book. Thanks also to Nigel Dunnett for his input on Sheffield Grey to Green. A huge thank you to the RHS for trusting me with this title, especially Dr Mark Gush, whose knowledge of waterwise gardening helped shape its content to align with the RHS's mission to "enrich lives through plants and create a greener world".

Finally, thanks to my mother who connected me with nature from childhood – a gift I will in turn pass on to my son. My hope is that this book encourages others to view water as a precious resource, to be valued and protected for future generations.

PUBLISHER'S ACKNOWLEDGEMENTS

Dorling Kindersley would like to thank Marc Redmile-Gordon, Senior Scientist for Soil and Climate Change at the RHS, for his invaluable advice; Vanessa Bird for indexing; Kathy Steer for proofreading; and Adam Brackenbury for repro work.

Senior Designer Barbara Zuniga
Senior Editor Alastair Laing
Publishing Assistant Emily Cannings
Senior Production Editor Tony Phipps
Senior Production Controller Stephanie McConnell
Editorial Director Ruth O'Rourke
Art Director Maxine Pedliham
Publishing Director Stephanie Jackson

Editorial Jo Whittingham
Design Vicky Read
Illustration Michael Powell (CGI), Andrew Torrens
Picture Research Emily Hedges
Design Styling Concept Alex Hunting Studio
Jacket Concept Work Eleanor Ridsdale

FOR THE RHS
Head of Environmental Horticulture Dr Mark Gush
Editor Simon Maughan
RHS Books Publisher Helen Griffin
Head of Editorial Tom Howard

First published in Great Britain in 2025 by
Dorling Kindersley Limited
20 Vauxhall Bridge Road,
London SW1V 2SA

The authorised representative in the EEA is
Dorling Kindersley Verlag GmbH. Arnulfstr. 124,
80636 Munich, Germany

Text copyright © Tom Massey 2025
Copyright © 2025 Dorling Kindersley Limited
A Penguin Random House Company
10 9 8 7 6 5 4 3 2 1
001–345505–Sep/2025

All rights reserved.
No part of this publication may be reproduced, stored in or introduced into a retrieval system, or transmitted, in any form, or by any means (electronic, mechanical, photocopying, recording, or otherwise), without the prior written permission of the copyright owner.

No part of this publication may be used or reproduced in any manner for the purpose of training artificial intelligence technologies or systems. In accordance with Article 4(3) of the DSM Directive 2019/790, DK expressly reserves this work from the text and data mining exception.

A CIP catalogue record for this book
is available from the British Library.
ISBN: 978-0-2417-4022-4

Printed and bound in China

www.dk.com

This book was made with Forest Stewardship Council™ certified paper – one small step in DK's commitment to a sustainable future. Learn more at www.dk.com/uk/information/sustainability

ABOUT THE AUTHOR

Tom Massey is an award-winning landscape designer and principal at Tom Massey Studio, a London-based practice renowned for pioneering sustainable and ecologically responsive landscapes. His portfolio includes private gardens, commercial spaces, and public realm projects, all unified by a commitment to enhance biodiversity, create ecosystem resilience, and build in adaptability to a changing climate.

A popular presence at the RHS Chelsea Flower Show, Tom has designed and exhibited four gardens: in 2024, the WaterAid Garden (with Studio Weave) was awarded an RHS Gold Medal; this followed an RHS Gold Medal and the BBC People's Choice Award in 2021, for the Yeo Valley Organic Garden, which showcased organic gardening principles; and, in 2018, an RHS Silver-Gilt Medal for the Lemon Tree Trust Garden, highlighting the therapeutic power of gardens in refugee communities.

In 2020, Tom's design for the "Hothouse" installation at the London Design Festival, in collaboration with Studio Weave, created an immersive vision of London's projected climate future. Designs for residential landscapes, all blending beauty with ecological function, have garnered Tom further awards, and he has also brought this philosophy to a wider audience as a featured designer on the BBC television series *Your Garden Made Perfect*.

Tom's books both mirror his design ethos and draw on research from the RHS science team. *RHS Resilient Garden*, offers a comprehensive approach to climate-adaptive garden design, while *RHS Waterwise Garden* serves as a guide to creating beautiful, water-efficient gardens that will thrive in our changing climate.